REAL ESTATE BUYING/SELLING GUIDE FOR OREGON

Fred A. Granata, Attorney

Self-Counsel Press Inc.
a subsidiary of

International Self-Counsel Press Ltd.
Canada   U.S.A.
(Printed in Canada)

Printed in Canada
First edition: January, 1980
Second edition: March, 1990

Canadian Cataloguing in Publication Data

Granata, Fred, A., 1931-
  Real estate buying/selling guide for Oregon

  (Self-counsel legal series)
  ISBN 0-88908-828-4

  1. Vendors and purchasers — Oregon — Popular works.
  2. House buying — Oregon.   3. House selling — Oregon.
  I. Title.   II. Series.
  KF02526.Z9G72   1990   346.79504'37   C90-091069-0

Self-Counsel Press Inc.
a subsidiary of
International Self-Counsel Press Ltd.
Head and Editorial Office
1481 Charlotte Road
North Vancouver, British Columbia, Canada V7J 1H1

U.S. Address
1704 N. State Street
Bellingham, Washington 98225

*This book is dedicated to my many friends who,
by their confidence in me, have enabled me to obtain
the experience and knowledge necessary to write it.*

CONTENTS

LIST OF SAMPLES

INTRODUCTION

I have been interested in the subject of real estate since I was a teenager. I used to work in a library. Part of my job was to get old volumes of newspapers from the stacks for customers. In the process I would observe advertisements of many years earlier. In 1916, lots in some of the better locations of Portland were selling for only a few hundred dollars. I used to think, "Why could I not have been around to take advantage of those prices?" Little did I realize that these early opportunities were still available but with different mathematical multiples. Because I like bargains, and for other reasons, the subject of real estate has continued to absorb me. As an attorney, I devote most of my professional time to that subject.

I intend not to advise on investment or to counsel the professional. I want to help the layperson unacquainted with real estate and perhaps approaching the subject for the first time. In the first part of this book, I take a seller and a buyer through the intricacies of a real estate transaction and try to make it more meaningful. I warn of some of the dangers and pitfalls.

In the second part, my object, then, is to stay with the owner because of different dangers and pitfalls he or she must then confront. How can the land be used? Can it be divided? What about a neighbor's fence? Or trees? There are literally thousands of questions created by the ownership of land.

In his brilliant book, *The Territorial Imperative*, Robert Ardrey makes the point that the desire to own an exclusive territory is found not only in humans but also in animals such as birds, wolves, and rodents. He suggests that in humans this is an instinct as strong as the instinct for life and mating, and that this instinct was genetically instilled into all animals.

It is little wonder, therefore, that humans have surrounded the ownership of land with such intricate rules. Just consider the synonym of land, the word "realty." Notice how it resembles the word "royalty." These words have a common derivation which gives us a pretty good idea how important our society considers land.

I should mention that this is not a book on social studies or history; nor is it a book on "how to do it yourself." There is no way I can set forth rules to fit all possible situations. I firmly believe that in matters of major importance (as I regard the sale and purchase of land), a person should be guided by a professional. I have known many attorneys and realtors, all knowledgeable and experienced negotiators, who found the sale of their own home to be overwhelming. The reason is lack of detachment. It is difficult to have sufficient objectivity about your own home. There is simply no substitute for the judgment and experience of a skilled attorney in legal matters and a skilled realtor in real estate matters. If you hire professionals, this book should give you a better insight into what they are saying and doing: if you are selling your home without professional help, it should provide you with a foundation and some of the tools.

Throughout this book I have used trade slang of the real estate industry. Wherever I have done this, I have also used the non-industry form to help you understand words you are likely to hear. While I do not provide a glossary of terms (because usually hardly anyone reads it), I will define one very basic term, real estate. Real estate is land and anything attached to it. This definition may be hard to apply in some situations; but for most it will suffice.

1

SHOULD YOU BUY A HOME?

Oregon has traditionally been a place where people owned their own homes. Portland was called a city of homes for many years. Its first apartment was not built until 1904 (on S.W. 16th and Jefferson), and it was not until the 1950s that apartments started to gain acceptance.

Prices in Oregon have been lower than the prices of comparable houses in many parts of the United States, but prices are going up. In early 1989, the median price of new one-family houses in the Portland area was $76,000. By December, 1989, the median had increased to $84,000. This is a significant increase. Many experts expect that the median will continue to go up until it is more in line with comparable situated areas. Prices for used housing are trailing those of new housing, but the trend is also upward.

a. HOW MUCH TO SPEND

The Department of Housing and Urban Development estimates that in 1970 half the people in the U.S. could have afforded to buy a median-priced new house — then $23,400 — by the normal credit rule that they spend no more than 25% of their pretax income on mortgage payments. Today, that standard has increased to 28% to 29% of pretax income. Many persons today simply cannot afford a new home.

How do you decide, then, how much of your income to put into a house?

Unless a seller intends to "carry the contract," the buyer is going to be required to find some lending institution to pay off the seller in full, so you must also ask "how much of my income will the lender *allow* me to commit to a house?"

1

The lender will look carefully at your income and assets. Lenders are generally mortgage companies, banks, mutual savings banks, savings and loan associations, and the like. It is most important to shop around for the best interest rate possible. This is one of the first ways that a savings can be made.

The lender uses several rules to estimate whether or not a buyer has sufficient income or salary to buy a home in a certain price range. Each institution applies these rules somewhat differently, so there *is* flexibility in structuring your financial package.

The first rule, which is now used almost exclusively by lending institutions, is the 33% rule (or the gross income rule). With this rule, you look at the outstanding debts which will not be paid off in 6 to 7 months or more, (e.g., the car payment). You add these outstanding debts to the payments on the new house. The total should not be more than 33% of your *gross* income. The house payment will include the principal, interest, taxes, and insurance (P+I+T+I).

The next rule specifies that the purchaser should not pay more than 28% of his or her *net* monthly income for a mortgage payment. This payment will generally include principal, interest, taxes, and insurance (P+I+T+I) on the home. Because of present day economies, this rule is now seldom used because it no longer gives a true picture of the purchaser's income. If the lending institution does apply this rule, it still deducts any large debts owed by the prospective purchaser, such as payments for an automobile, a piece of furniture, or a television.

A third rule is the 2-1/2 times formula. This rule, which is also seldom used, provides that the purchase price of the house should not exceed 2-1/2 times the purchaser's gross income. For example, if your gross annual salary is $25,000, you should be able to purchase a home for $62,000 ($25,000 x 2.5 = $62,500).

Keep in mind that none of these formulas is applied rigidly. Consideration is also given to other factors, such as:

(a) Length and stability of employment

(b) Job skills and demand for them

(c) Other income such as bonuses, interest, and dividends

(d) Credit history, status, and rating

(e) Source of down payment, with greater weight being given to savings and no weight being given to borrowed money

(f) Remaining cash after down payment

The lender must look at the risk involved. However, these formulas give you some indication of how much you can afford to spend on the purchase of a home. Using these, you can understand what a lender will consider in determining whether or not to lend money to you.

In the past, if a couple applied for a mortgage, it was common for the lender to consider only the male spouse's income when determining eligibility. Today, federal law dictates that lenders must take into account the income of both spouses and whether the spouses are married is not a proper question for the lender to ask. Laws of this kind bind only commercial lenders, not an individual who is selling his or her home on an installment basis.

b. PURCHASE A HOME AT MAXIMUM LIMIT — TWO POINTS OF VIEW

It should be mentioned at this point that there is some justification for attempting to purchase a home at the outer limits of your income. The thinking behind this is that in periods of inflation you will be earning more money, which will be available to "catch up" with the monthly mortgage payment. Also, family incomes are rising.

But you should use this philosophy with some caution. A crisis such as an illness or an unusual expense could result in the failure to make the payments, which could result in a foreclosure of the home or, at least, added expenses in attempting to prevent foreclosure or forfeiture of the home.

With these ideas in mind, you, the buyer, can now proceed to other concerns in your attempt to purchase a house.

2

HOW TO LOOK FOR A HOUSE

a. GENERAL

You should first decide the general area where you would like to live, and look for a house there. It will come as no surprise to learn that the same or similar house in one area will be priced higher than in another area. This is because some neighborhoods or residential areas are higher priced than others. When you stop to consider it, not only do you buy a home for comfort, convenience, security, and other intangible reasons, but also as an investment for the time when you eventually decide to sell. Some homes, because of their location and agreeable surroundings, may initially cost more, but may appreciate faster and be worth more when you sell.

1. Location

A knowledgeable real estate agent can help you select a location that will best suit your needs. This agent can also help you select a home in a neighborhood that should continue to increase in value. As a buyer, using an agent in this way is good business practice because it is the seller, not the buyer, who is obligated to pay the real estate commission.

In choosing your location, you should consider such factors as the distance from your work, the proximity to bus routes, the distance from, and quality of, the schools in the neighborhood, the proximity to stores and shopping areas, the location and number of parks and swimming pools, and the proximity to major streets and freeways.

In these days of high gasoline prices when the emphasis is on energy conservation, it is important to consider the distance to your work. If the distance from your future home to your place of work is greater than the distance you

5

now travel, think carefully about the time you have to spend driving to and from work in bumper to bumper traffic with a gasoline bill even larger than the one you complain about now. You should also consider how close you are to bus routes and how often they operate. You, your spouse, and your children may find it necessary or convenient to take the bus on some regular basis.

If you have a school-age child, you might consider whether you will have to drive the child to and from school every day because of a dangerous highway between your home and school. All of these considerations, and others which may be unique to your situation, should be considered in determining whether the location in which you are interested serves your needs, or whether it will place an undue burden upon your standard of living.

2. View

It hardly needs repeating that people like view property. But view property is expensive because it has an aesthetic appeal which makes it more desirable. All things being equal, view property should appreciate faster and be worth more when you finally decide to sell it.

But a word of caution. You should also thoroughly investigate the present zoning regulations, including any prospective zoning changes in the area. You should determine whether your view might be cut off by future construction of other houses or buildings in the neighborhood. If this happens, the value of your house could suffer, and most likely you would have no recourse.

You should also investigate the neighborhood itself to determine whether or how your view would become restricted through normal building by other lot owners or by the growth of large trees.

3. Average-priced house

It is generally not a good idea to purchase the most expensive house in a neighborhood. Houses tend to be appraised on the basis of a comparison with the surrounding houses. If some homeowners tend to let their places deteriorate, the value of your high-priced home cannot avoid being affected in some degree. To be safe, you should buy a home priced somewhere in the middle range of the neighborhood. In that way, the value of your home should continue to reflect the value of the other homes within the neighborhood.

On the other hand, if you find a fix-up home at a bargain price in an otherwise good residential neighborhood, you may want to consider buying it. By doing some of the work yourself and contracting out the other work, you will not only increase the value of your home, but you may well increase the value of the neighborhood. This in turn will be to your benefit since your house will increase in value as values in the neighborhood rise.

Nevertheless, if you decide to buy one of the most expensive houses in the neighborhood, you should satisfy yourself that the neighborhood is a stable one, and is likely to remain that way in the foreseeable future. In that way you will have protected yourself against the possible depreciation of your investment because of neighborhood deterioration.

4. Zoning

People buy homes to live in them, raise a family, and entertain relatives, guests, and friends: in short, for residential purposes. The home is a retreat, a place to relax and enjoy yourself. Most people buy a home for these reasons, and more. This is why it is important to discover how zoning might affect your prospective residence. While you are still contemplating the purchase of the house, take a walk around the neighborhood. Are there industrial plants on the next corner? Are there commercial buildings down the street? Is there a gas station or a busy apartment across the street? These kinds of places could depress the value of your property.

How stable do you think the residential neighborhood will remain? An unstable area will affect your property values, and so will noise, heavy traffic, dust, and smoke.

7

You should try to determine how long the area will remain the way you want it to be. Unless you are buying with the intention of later selling for commercial purposes, you should pause to consider whether the purchase of this property as your home will suit your needs.

If the area is zoned residential, try to determine from the local zoning agency, as well as from people in the neighborhood, whether the residential zoning classification is likely to change in the near future. Encroachments from light business, stores, gas stations, apartments, and the like, could seriously affect the value of your prospective property.

In walking around the neighborhood, observe how the neighbors keep up their homes. Is the grass well kept? Are the homes painted and well maintained? Have trees and flowers been planted to add to the beauty and value of the homes? If so, you may feel comfortable in the realization that this appears to be a very stable neighborhood.

In summary, take your time in looking for the right home. Examine the location, check the zoning, and look at the other homes in the neighborhood. If you can say you would like to live there, you have at least selected the type of neighborhood to look in.

3
SELLING YOUR HOUSE

a. THE REAL ESTATE BROKER

When you decide to sell your house, you will probably list it with a real estate broker. This is a person who has passed an examination, has been licensed by the state, and is subject to audit and regulation by the state. Brokers will charge (usually on a commission basis) to sell your property. Anyone who sells another's property without charge is not a real estate broker under Oregon law.

The term "realtor" is often used erroneously to mean a real estate broker, but this is a coined and trademarked term, and refers only to a person who is a member of and who has subscribed to the code of ethics of a realty board, a private professional organization. A broker may or may not be a realtor.

b. THE LISTING AGREEMENT

When you sell through a real estate broker, you will usually be asked to sign a listing agreement (see Samples #1 and #2). This is only valid if it is in writing and contains the description of the property (a street address is sufficient). Study it carefully.

All listing agreements (called "listings") should contain these essential terms:

(a) A description of the property
(b) The price
(c) The terms of sale
(d) The duration of the agreement
(e) The agreed commission

It must also provide for where the earnest money goes if the deal falls through. It should be signed by the owners of

9

the property and the broker or the broker's representative. The listing does not authorize the broker or salesperson to sign the deed or contract of sale; only the owner can sign these documents. It authorizes them only to find a buyer. If you give a listing to a particular broker, only that broker and his or her salespeople are legally and ethically permitted to show your property.

The listing agreement is a contract and once you sign it you are bound by its terms for the period of time set out in the agreement. The contract entitles the listing agent to demand the minimum fee payable should you withdraw from the listing agreement before its expiration date.

As a practical matter, should you for some reason wish to do this, you should talk your predicament over with the broker. If the reason for wanting to withdraw is legitimate, most brokers will be understanding and will make a businesslike agreement. Commonly they will ask you to pay their out-of-pocket expenses such as advertising and multiple listing costs. They will ask you to agree not to re-list the house until after 120 days, and that if you do re-list it within a year, that you do it with the same broker. These last two requirements are imposed to determine the sincerity of your reason for cancellation and to give the broker and his or her salespeople at least a chance to get payment for the efforts they have made.

One thing should be said concerning the duration of the listing. Most listing agreements contain a provision which extends the duration date for a certain number of days after the written expiration date but this applies only to someone the broker has shown the property to before the expiration date of the listing. Brokers do this to protect themselves from sellers who utilize their services to procure a buyer without paying for them.

The "standard" real estate commission, that charged by the majority of Oregon brokers, is 7% of the sales price. This is generally true whether you list with one broker or within a multiple listing service, or whether the sale is a "co-op."

When choosing a real estate broker, consider everything you can find out about the broker's company.

What services does it offer?

Is it a member of a multiple listing service?

Does it have an equity advance program? (This enables you to borrow on your equity if you need funds right away.)

Is it a member of any professional associations?

Does it have a sales training program for its personnel?

What is its advertising policy?

Does it offer a relocation service?

Is there a "guaranteed" sales program? (If your real estate qualifies, the broker will buy your house from you for a stated price according to an agreed formula if he or she cannot sell it.)

Is there a closing coordinator? (This person is of great help in assuring fast and efficient closing of the sale.)

What is the geographic area generally served by the broker?

What is the broker's emphasis? Is it residential? commercial? or is it land development?

Do real estate professionals, builders and the like, use the broker's services?

A broker has performed his or her obligations and is entitled to a commission under the listing agreement when a buyer who is ready, willing, and able to purchase the property under the terms of the listing agreement is presented to you, the seller. A buyer who is willing to pay less than the listing price or who wants to buy on terms other than cash or whose offer does not conform to even one of the listing terms is not considered to be a buyer who is ready, willing, and able. An offer like this does not obligate you to pay a commission unless you accept the offer. Nor are you obligated to pay a commission where the buyer later withdraws (perhaps illicitly) from the transaction (called a "sale fail"). This risk is borne by the broker.

1. The exclusive agreement

The most common type of listing agreement is the exclusive agreement which specifies a period of time (most commonly 90 days) during which there is only one real estate broker who can sell the property (see Sample #1). If your house is sold during that period, the broker is entitled to the agreed commission even if you make the sale yourself. However, you do not have to sign an exclusive listing agreement; and if you do, you can always include a clause reserving the right to sell yourself without paying a commission to the broker.

2. Multiple listing

In today's real estate market, the competition is not only to sell a house but also to get listings. Consequently, there has developed what are called multiple listing services (called "multiple" in the trade). Various of these services exist in the larger metropolitan areas of Oregon.

A multiple listing service is essentially a cooperative of real estate brokers, all of whom have access to the listings of other members. These brokers have arrangements for sharing the commission and the conduct of business between two brokers. The broker who gets the listing is called the listing broker, and the one who sells, the selling broker. One broker, of course, may be both the listing and the selling broker. Under the rules of multiple listing, only the listing broker is allowed to transact business with the seller, his or her client.

SAMPLE #1
EXCLUSIVE LISTING AGREEMENT

No. 674 © Rev. TT
Stevens-Ness L.P.Co.
Portland, OR 9720/

REAL ESTATE BROKER'S   **EMPLOYMENT CONTRACT**   RESIDENCE PROPERTY

DESCRIPTION: _Lot 3, Block 2, PLEASANT PARK_
commonly known as 2022 S. E. Green Street
(If said property is incorrectly described, owner hereby expressly authorizes broker subsequently to write in hereon or attach hereto, the correct legal description thereof.)

City of _Portland_, County of _Multnomah_, State of _Oregon_ Zip _97268_; for better description see owner's title deed on record, now made a part hereof. For personal property, if any to be included in property offered for sale next mentioned. See below or see signed inventory, to be attached.

Selling price, free of encumbrances: $_65,000_, Terms _Cash_

Is any personal propery included in this listing? Yes ☐; No ☒ if so, is signed inventory attached? Yes ☐; No ☐; to be attached? Yes ☐; No ☐.

To _We Sellum Realtors_ Broker, City _Portland_ State _Oregon_ _January 1_, 19 90
FOR VALUE RECEIVED, you hereby are employed to sell or exchange the property described hereon at the selling price and the terms stated. You hereby are authorized to accept a deposit on the purchase price. You may, if desired, secure the cooperation of any other broker, or group of brokers, in procuring a sale of said property. In the event that you, or any other brokers cooperating with you, shall find a buyer ready and willing to enter into a deal for said price and terms, or such other terms and price as I may accept, or that during your employment you supply me with the name of or place me in contact with a buyer to or through whom at any time within 90 days after the termination of said employment I may

sell or convey said property, I hereby agree to pay you in cash for your services a commission equal to _____% of the above stated selling price. I agree to convey said real estate to the purchaser by a good and sufficient deed, to transfer said personal property, if any, by good and sufficient bill of sale and to furnish title insurance in the amount of the selling price insuring marketable title to said real estate and good right to convey. I hereby warrant that the information shown hereon below is true, that I am the owner of said property, that my title thereto is a good and marketable title, that the same is free of encumbrances except as shown hereafter under "Financial Details" and except taxes levied on said property for the current tax year which are to be pro rated between the seller and buyer. In case of an exchange, I have no objection to your representing and accepting compensation from the other party to the exchange as well as myself. I hereby authorize you and your customers to enter any part of said property at any reasonable time to show same. Also, I authorize you, at any time, to fill in and complete all or any part of the "Informative Data" below, except financial details. The following items are to be left upon the premises as part of the property purchased: All irrigation, plumbing, ventilating, cooling and heating fixtures and equipment (including stoker and oil tanks but excluding fire place fixtures and equipment), water heaters, attached electric light and bath room fixtures, light bulbs and fluorescent lamps, venetian blinds, wall-to-wall carpeting, awnings, window and door screens, storm doors and windows, attached floor coverings, attached television antenna, all plants, shrubs and trees and all fixtures except _None_

The following personal property is also included as a part of the property to be offered for sale for said price: _None_

(or see signed inventory, if any, attached). This agreement expires at midnight on _March 31_, 19 90, but I further allow you a reasonable time thereafter to close any deal on which earnest money is then deposited. In case of suit or action on this contract, it is agreed between us that the trial and appellate courts may allow the prevailing party therein such sum as may be adjudged that party's reasonable attorney's fees. It is further agreed that my signature affixed to the renewal clause below shall have the effect of renewing and extending your employment to a new date to be fixed by me on the same terms and all with the same effect as if the said new date had been fixed above as the expiration date of your employment. Disposition of forfeited earnest money, if any, to be negotiated and set forth in the Earnest Money Receipt (Oregon only, delete if inapplicable).
*THIS LISTING IS AN EXCLUSIVE LISTING and you hereby are granted the absolute, sole and exclusive right to sell or exchange the said described property. In the event of any sale, by me or any other person, or of exchange or conveyance of said property, or any part thereof, during the term of your exclusive employment, or in case I withdraw the authority hereby given prior to said expiration date, I agree to pay you the said commission just the same as if a sale had actually been consummated by you.
I HEREBY CERTIFY THAT I HAVE READ AND RECEIVED A CARBON COPY OF THIS CONTRACT.

Accepted: _January 1_, 19 _90_   _Sam Seller_ Owner
L. Listing Broker   Owner
Owner's Address _123 S. E. Quiet Street_ City _Portland_ State _Oregon_ Zip _97239_ Phone _999-3827_

FOR VALUE RECEIVED, the above broker's employment hereby is renewed and extended to and including _____, 19____.
Accepted: _____, 19____   Owner
Broker   Owner
- - - - FOLD ON DOTTED LINE FOR INSERTION IN RING BINDER - - - -

FINANCIAL DETAILS

Selling price (free of encumbrances)
$_65,000_ Terms _Cash_

Payments include: Prin. ___ Int. ___ Taxes ___ Ins. ___
(Check items to be included in payments)
Interest on deferred payments ____%
Fire ins. $ ____ Ann'l prem. $ ____
Taxes last fiscal year $ ____
F.H.A. commitment $ ____

ENCUMBRANCES   Payable
1st mtg. $ _22,000_ Int. _10_ % _month_
2nd mtg. $ ____ Int. ____%
Mtg. held by ____
Contr. bal. $ ____ Int. ____%
Delinquent taxes $ ____
Municipal liens $ ____

	B	1F	2F	A	Comment
Living rm.		X			15X30
Dining rm.		X			10X15
Family rm.	X				15X30
Kitchen		X			15X20
Bedrms.	4	10X20	10X12		
Bath	2				6X10
Den					
Party rm.					
Utility rm.		X			10X12
Hallway		X			6X8
Eat Space		X			10X8

Attic: No Fin. ____ Unfin. ____

RESIDENCE PROPERTY INFORMATIVE DATA

Office Listing No. _5200_

Address _2022 S. E. Green Street_
Betw _20th_ and _22nd_ Dist _PLEASANT HOMES_
Lot _3_ Block _2_ Addn _PLEASANT PARK_ Facing _N_ S X _E___ W___
No. stories _2_ size lot _100_ x _100_ Size house _50_ x _40_ Sq. _2000_
Owner has Title Insurance _Yes_ Abstract ____ Contract ____ Deed ____
Occupied by: Owner ____ Vacant X Renter ____ Renter's name ____ Tel ____ Rent $ ____
Owner's name _Sam Seller_ Tel ____
May we use pass key _Yes_ Key at _Broker_
Possession may be had _one day after closing_
Type of house _2 story colonial_
Type of construction _wood frame_ Type of roof ____
Condition Roof _good_ Paint exterior _good_ Paint interior _good_
Utilities: Electricity _yes_ Gas _yes_ Phone _yes_ Water _yes_ Garbage service _yes_
For details as to chattels included in sale See employment contract _n/a_ See signed inventory ____

FEATURES & FINISH	HEATING & COOLING	OUTSIDE	DISTANCE TO
Sink _stainless_	House _gas_	Garage: Single ___ Dbl ___	Bus _4 blocks_
Dishwasher _Kitchenaid_		Carport _Yes_	Name of line _Slow_
Disposal _No_		Lawn _Good_	Grade School _3 blocks_
Laundry Trays _2_		Garden _Flower_	High School _10 blocks_
Shower _throughout_		Shrubbery _Yes_	Pub. Park _10 blocks_
Fir floor ____		Sprinkler ____	Grocery store _10 blocks_
Hdwd. floor _throughout_			MISCELLANEOUS
W/W Carpeting _kitchen_	Water ____		Sewer _Yes_
Vinyl floors _kitchen_		STREETS	Cesspool ____
Plaster ceiling _Yes_	BASEMENT	Paved _Yes_	Outdoor frplce ____ Sep. tank _No_
Beam ceiling ____	Full X Part ___	Macadam ____	Walks ____
Rooms papered ____	Fin ___ Unfin ___	Graded ____	Weatherstripping _Yes_
Rooms tinted _3_	Floor Drain ____	Ungraded ____	Insulation: Ceil. X Wall X
Enamel finish _3_		Sidewalk _Yes_	Blt. in Rng ____ Oven ____
Natural finish ____		Alley _No_	Wired elect. stove _X_

Remarks: _Leaded glass windows in dining room; window seat in hall_

Listed by _L. Listing_
Signs permitted _Yes_
Inspected by ____

Will consider exchange for _No_

* TO MAKE NON-EXCLUSIVE - Strike complete paragraph following asterisk (*) in Employment Contract and have owner initial deletion.

BROKER'S COPY

SAMPLE #2
MULTIPLE LISTING AGREEMENT

OREGON MULTIPLE LISTING SERVICE
RESIDENTIAL LISTING FORM

☒ RESIDENTIAL ☐ TOWNHOUSE / CONDO
☐ MOBILE HOMES ☐ HOUSEBOATS

FOR OMLS USE ONLY
OMLS LISTING

OFFICE LISTING #

PRICE	LIST DATE	EXPIRE DATE	CODIFIED CO-OP INFO†	TOTAL SQ. FT.	MAIN FLR. SQ. FT.	SUBAREA CODE ★
65,000	01,01,90	03,30,90		2000	1100	00

Address: 2022 S.E. Green Street   City Code 4X   X-Street 20th - 22nd Ave.

Occupied by: ☒ Owner ☐ Vacant ☐ Renter   Renter's Name: _____   Phone 389-2222   Lot Size 100x100

Show: ☒ Appt. Only ☐ By Appt., but if no answer Use Lkbx ☐ Lkbx   Lockbox Location ☐ Door ☐ Rail ☒ Faucet

Possession to be delivered 30 days after recording or NA   Neighborhood Pleasant Park

Main	Up	Down	ROOM SIZES	Basement 100 %	Age # 12 years	Terms 5,000
X			Entry 6x8	Style ranch	Levels 2 +bsmt.	Add'l Terms
X			Living Rm. 15x30	Exterior shakes	Sewer ☒ Yes	Loan Balance $60,000
X			Dining Rm. 10x15	Roof cedar shingle	Connected ☒ Yes	Payment $ 600 per mo. @ 9 %
X			Kitchen 15x20	Heat gas furnace	Septic ☐ Yes	Loan # NA PITI
			Eat Space 10x8	Fireplace brick	Cesspool ☐ Yes	Owed To NA
		X	Family Rm. 15x30	Insulation 6"fiberglass	Fenced Cedar	Assumption Fee $ NA @ 5 %
		X	Utility Rm. 10x20	Built-Ins ☒Yes	Floors W W Carpet	Pay Off Fee $ NA
# 1 # 2 #	Baths 6x10		Garage carport	Water City	Additional Encumbrance $ None per yr.
# 4 #	Bedrooms Master 10x20, others 10x12					Taxes 1527

Grade School 3 Blks   Junior Hi 10 Blks   Senior Hi 10 Blks   Parochial 1/2 mile   Sch Bus ☒Yes

Warranty & Other Exceptions: roof is 2 years old; newly painted   Blocks to City Bus 3

Owner Sam Seller   Address 2020 S.E. Green   Bus Ph 255-8453   Hm Ph 765-4321   SPECIAL INFORMATION

Legal/Remarks/Inclusions: Association Fee $ None

Listing Office We Sellum Realtor   Includes

LO # 4   Ph # 255-8953   Title to Land: ☒ Yes ☐ No

Slsp # 6   Ph #

LAND SIZE: Pool ☐ Yes   View ☒ Yes   Waterfront ☐ Yes
☒ Standard Lot ☐ Large Lot ☐ Small Lot ☐ Acreage   If Acreage, How Many Acres?

ALL ITEMS IN "BOLD FACE TYPE" ARE DATA INPUT ITEMS. PLEASE VERIFY ACCURACY.   *REFER TO SUBAREA MAPS FRONT OF OMLS BOOK
†Only insert codified information from inside back cover of weekly book.

TO We Sellum Realtor   For value received, you are hereby employed and given the exclusive right to sell or exchange the above
described property at the price and terms stated above. You are hereby authorized to accept a deposit or any part of the purchase price and hold it in your client's trust account or place it in an
escrow established for closing the sale of said property. In the event that you, or any other broker cooperating with you, find a buyer ready and willing to purchase said property for said price
and terms, or such other price and terms as I may accept, or in the event of any sale, contract to sell or exchange or conveyance of said property during the life of this contract or any renewal
or extension thereof, or that you place me in touch with a buyer to whom at any time within ninety days after the termination of this contract or renewal or extension thereof I may sell, contract
to sell or exchange or convey said property, or if you are the procuring cause of said sale, exchange or conveyance, I hereby agree to pay you in cash for your services in connection with this
contract a fee equal in amount to seven % of the selling price of the property, but in no case less than $ 500
Except as provided above I warrant: (1) that I am the owner of said property or the authorized agent to act for the owner; (2) that the information given above is true and correct; (3) that the
above described property is free of all encumbrances except taxes for the current fiscal year which are to be prorated; (4) that my title thereto is a good marketable title; (5) that as of the date
buyer is entitled to possession the real and personal property listed including structural, electrical, heating, cooling and plumbing systems will be in good operating condition and free of material
defects; (6) that there are no violations of any laws or regulations relating to that property; (7) that I have no knowledge of any lien to be assessed against that property. I agree to defend and
indemnify you, your officers, agents and subagents against any claim whether or not frivolous, connected with breach of any of the foregoing warranties or with my failure to disclose any material
facts or with alleged defects or conditions of which you had no knowledge. I agree to convey said real property to the purchaser by a good and sufficient deed and to furnish title insurance and
to transfer and deliver said personal property if any, by a good and sufficient bill of sale. In case of an exchange, I have no objection to your representing and accepting compensation from the
other party to the exchange as well as myself. I understand you are a subscriber to Oregon Multiple Listing Service (OMLS) and you are hereby authorized to place this listing in that service and
to publish, use and furnish to OMLS for publication and use any offer or sales data or information you or any cooperating broker becomes aware of in connection with marketing of the property.
I understand that you cooperate with other brokers and that they may act in procuring or attempting to procure a purchaser for said property under the terms of this agreement. I hereby authorize
you and your customers and sales cooperating brokers and their customers to enter any part of said property at any reasonable time to inspect same and you are authorized to place a lockbox and
a for sale sign on said property. I allow you a reasonable time after termination of this contract to close any sale or exchange on which earnest money is then deposited. In case I withdraw the
authority hereby given during the term of this contract, I agree to pay the said fee just as if a sale had been consummated. In case of suit or action on this contract, I agree to pay such additional
sum as the court may adjudge reasonable as your attorneys fees in said suit or action and appeal thereof.
  The following items are to be left upon the premises as part of the property to be purchased: all irrigation fixtures and equipment, plumbing and heating fixtures and equipment, electric
light fixtures, light bulbs and fluorescent tubes, curtain rods, drapery rods, valances, venetian blinds, window and door screens, storm doors and windows, attached fireplace screens and equipment, attached TV antenna, all shrubs and trees, and all items that are affixed by nail or screw, and all fixtures except
Built in cabinet in dining room, ornamental maple in front garden

The term of this exclusive listing commences on the 1st day of August, 19 89, and expires at midnight on Tuesday,
the 30th day of October, 19 89.

I hereby authorize any lender or contract vendor with respect to the real property described above, to release to any broker or sales associate subscribing to OMLS, any information
regarding the loan or contract that such broker or sales associate may request.

In consideration of the above, we agree to endeavor to effect a sale or exchange
in accordance with the terms and conditions set forth.

I (SELLER) HEREBY ACKNOWLEDGE I HAVE RECEIVED AND FULLY READ AND
UNDERSTAND A COMPLETELY FILLED-IN COPY OF THIS AGREEMENT. In the event
that a prospective purchaser makes a deposit or pays any part of the purchase price of the
property and thereafter forfeits the same or any part thereof, you are authorized in my
name, or otherwise, to declare such forfeiture. The amount forfeited after deduction of
any title insurance or escrow cancellation charges shall be distributed as follows:
☐ To you, to the extent of the agreed commission, just as if the transaction had been
consummated, with residue to me; or

We Sellum Realtors   ☒ to be divided 50-50 between the broker
Broker   and Sam Seller, seller.

By Larry Listing L. Listing   July 29, 1989   Sam Seller   July 29, 1989
REPRESENTATIVE   DATE   OWNER   DATE

THIS IS A LEGALLY BINDING CONTRACT. IF NOT UNDERSTOOD SEEK COMPETENT ADVICE.   Revised 2/79

Form OMLS-2C (Revised 2/79) PG
COPY DISTRIBUTION: Goldenrod to Owner — Pink to OMLS — Yellow to OMLS — White to Broker

14

Sample listing agreement — points to heed

The details about your house are fairly straightforward and should not cause you any trouble. However, you should read the fine print carefully and be sure you understand each part. The following comments will help to clarify the points in the listing which you agree to when you sign. The numbers correspond to the boldface numbers in Sample #2.

Note 1: If you sell your house to a purchaser introduced by the broker within 90 days of the terms of this contract, the broker gets a commission.

Note 2: You are encouraged to be honest and make full disclosure to the broker. If you fail to do so — if you don't mention those leaks in the roof or the fact that your fence trespasses on your neighbor's property — then you may have to defend the broker in a suit brought by a disappointed buyer. This is awkward: many brokers would rather not know about the ants in the attic as it makes it more difficult for them to sell.

Note 3: You, as seller, are responsible for furnishing title insurance.

Note 4: If you withdraw from the agreement before its expiry date, the broker is entitled to demand the minimum fee payable. You are also agreeing to pay reasonable attorney's fees for the broker in the event of a lawsuit arising from the listing agreement.

Note 5: Be sure to list here all the items you are taking with you out of your house that would otherwise be considered "fixtures" or attached to the land, such as built-in dishwashers, stoves, favorite shrubs, that special chandelier, and so on.

Note 6: Here you, the seller, are being invited to agree to forfeit part or all of a deposit on the purchase price to the broker in the event that the deal falls through. Alternatively, you can write in different terms, as has been done in this example.

If you list with a member of a multiple listing service, you are legally listed with the service, not the broker. The listing broker, who is still "your broker," and all the other members are sub-agents of the multiple listing service. A multiple listing service offers the advantage of giving your property more sales exposure. Its disadvantage is that it can cause you to do business with brokers and salespeople unknown to you. When you list your home, you have the right to insist that it not be placed in multiple, and conversely you have the right to have it placed there. Sample #2 shows the type of listing agreement you make when using a multiple listing service.

3. Cooperative transactions

A cooperative transaction (called a co-op) is similar to multiple listing but without the organizational formality. In this situation, a broker who does not have the listing or who is not a member of the multiple which has the listing requests permission of the listing broker to show your house to a prospective buyer. The "co-op broker" is then a sub-agent of your broker, the listing broker. This arrangement is usually entered into when your listing broker answers the question "Are you cooperating on the sale?" affirmatively. It is usually set up before the potential buyer is shown through the house.

4

THE EARNEST MONEY AGREEMENT

Usually, once a purchaser and seller agree on the sale of real estate the first document signed is an earnest money agreement or, as it sometimes is called, the earnest money receipt. But make no mistake about it, whether called an agreement or receipt, it is a contract between the purchaser and seller in every sense of the word. This chapter will concern itself only with those earnest money agreements (called "earnest money") which provide for a sale for cash. Those which call for a sale in installments will be covered in the chapter on financing.

In a broker sale the earnest money agreement usually starts its life with an offer from the buyer. The offer does not become an agreement until the seller accepts it. The buyer's offer is accompanied by a deposit in the form of cash, check, or note which should be payable on the seller's acceptance of the offer. This is the earnest money. The deposit is given to demonstrate that the buyer is serious, so much so that the money will be forfeited if, after the seller accepts the offer, the buyer does not complete the purchase.

a. HOW MUCH SHOULD THE DEPOSIT BE?

The first question is how large should the earnest deposit be? The answer to some extent depends upon the size of the transaction. The larger the sale price the more earnest money, proportionately, but there is no formula that will answer the question simply. The buyer wants it to be as small as possible, but large enough to be taken seriously; the seller wants it to be sufficiently large to discourage the buyer from forfeiting. As a rule of thumb, in the average residential sale, $1,000 earnest money is thought to be about right.

Once the offer is accepted, the property is taken off the market, and no seller or broker wants to do this without some reasonable assurance that the sale will go through. Other serious buyers might be lost.

Protect your own interests. Before accepting an offer, investigate and inquire about the buyer's qualifications — bona fide or just a wishful thinker? What is the buyer's credit rating? Does it look probable from all appearances that the buyer will qualify for financing? Your broker should be able to help you here.

b. FORFEITURE

What about forfeited earnest money if the buyer backs out of the offer? Oregon law now requires this to be negotiated with the owner and the disposition of it to be set out in either the listing or earnest money agreement. It usually appears in both of them (see Note 6 on Sample #2).

Commonly the agreement will provide that forfeited earnest money will be shared 50-50 between the seller and broker. This legislation, intended to benefit consumers, is somewhat unfortunate for buyers — a broker is more inclined to refund forfeited earnest money than a seller is.

Is the seller limited to claiming the earnest money or can a buyer in default be sued? Whether forfeiture of the earnest money is available to the seller depends upon the provisions of the agreement. Unfortunately, most earnest money agreements commonly in use are not written with such precision, and there is substantial doubt whether a seller can successfully sue the defaulting buyer for damages or to compel performance.

In most residential transactions, the seller is wiser to put aside the idea of suing a defaulting buyer and concentrate instead on reselling the property. The expense of such lawsuits usually outweighs any possible benefits. This is only general advice. In the specific case this question can be decided only by the seller and an attorney.

On the other side of the coin, what can the buyer do if the seller refuses to go through with the sale after accepting the offer in the earnest money agreement? Here the remedy is clearer because there is no problem with forfeiture of earnest money. The Oregon Supreme Court has declared that an earnest money agreement is a contract and may be specifically enforced, that is, the seller can be ordered by a court to complete the sale and transfer title to the buyer. Despite this ruling, some earnest money agreements are not sufficiently well written to be enforced in this way — though they should be, as that is in part what you are paying your broker for. Whether a buyer would want to sue in this situation is largely an economic decision. If a comparable residence is available for a similar price, the disgruntled buyer is usually better off attempting another purchase.

c. WHEN THE OFFER IS ACCEPTED

The buyer's offer does not become a contract unless the seller's acceptance conforms in every respect to the buyer's offer. If there is even the slightest difference in the seller's acceptance, it is not really an acceptance but a rejection and a counteroffer, and it is not binding.

This is not to say that the seller should not make a counteroffer as part of the negotiating process. This can be handled by the seller putting new and different terms on a separate page (often called an "addendum") and asking for the buyer's agreement to them. Sometimes it can be done by crossing out some things and writing in new terms on the offer document, acceptance being indicated by the other party's initials. While this method has been criticized by some people, it can be quite efficient if handled properly. Sellers and buyers should still exercise caution, however, as too many cross outs, initialed or not, or too many offers and counteroffers can create difficult interpretation questions. Sometimes it is better to start the document all over again from scratch. Your goal, after all, is to buy or sell the house, not plunge yourself into litigation.

What should a buyer consider before signing an earnest money agreement?

For one thing, you should be certain that everything you think you are buying is written into the earnest money agreement. The forms usually contain room for more than just the filling in of blanks and additional pages can always be added.

Most buyers, being unable to pay cash, must borrow from a lending institution. In this case, the earnest money agreement *must* specify that the purchase is contingent upon the buyer obtaining a loan (usually described as conventional, FHA, VA, FHA/VA, State, GI, etc.) to finance payment.

A buyer who wishes to be extremely careful should insist that the amount of the loan, the interest rate, and duration of payment be included as part of the contingency clause which appears in the earnest money agreement. Real estate salespeople generally do not include these terms in the belief that they usually make it easier for a buyer to escape the contract. In case of government financing, it is unnecessary to state them because these matters are set by law or regulation.

By placing the financing contingency in the earnest money agreement, the buyer is protected because if a loan cannot be obtained on the terms set out in the agreement, the transaction is terminated and the buyer is entitled to a refund of the earnest money deposit.

Often a buyer will make the earnest money agreement contingent upon the buyer's approval of a report by an inspection company. For a relatively small fee, these companies will examine a home looking for defects and needed repairs. Many commercial lenders will not give you a mortgage without viewing such an inspection report. If you do make your earnest money agreement contingent upon such an inspection and the report proves less than satisfactory, you will be able to back out of the purchase.

Another problem faces the buyer who owns a home and is looking for a replacement. Most buyers cannot afford to own two homes. What do they do? The solution is to add a provision that the purchase is contingent upon the sale of the buyer's present home, or that the purchase will close on sale of the buyer's present home. This requires, however, a great deal of coordination among all parties, buyers, sellers, lenders, brokers, escrow agents, and the like, especially when three or four of these are contingent on the others. Despite the problems involved this is a common occurrence.

But what if you are the seller? Do you want to take your home off the market because you have received an offer made on such a contingency? The buyer's home will usually be sold, but it could be months later. On the other hand, the buyer genuinely wants the house and is willing to pay top value.

The brokers have developed a tidy solution for this dilemma. It is called the "72 hour contingency" (see Sample #4). This is a supplemental document which forms part of the earnest money agreement and allows the seller to continue to try and sell the home. If a second and firm offer to buy is obtained, then the first buyer has 72 hours in which to eliminate the contingency clause in the original offer. If the contingency clause is not waived, the first transaction will be voided and the second transaction will be the effective one.

All these possibilities or contingencies must be disclosed on the earnest money agreements of all affected transactions. This can get quite complicated for the inexperienced person. Sometimes these complications are good business, but avoid them if at all possible, and if you can't — be careful. If in doubt, see your attorney ahead of time.

The date of possession must be mutually determined by buyer and seller. The buyer will want possession as soon as possible; the seller may want to delay in order to have time to move. This is an area that calls for fairness on both sides. A seller who is receiving full price can afford to be more generous and vacate quickly. Conversely, a buyer who is getting a bargain price should be willing to wait a little longer before taking possession.

There are a number of earnest money agreement forms. Some are printed commercially (see Sample #3); others are designed for use by the Oregon Association of Realtors and by the Realtors Association of Portland; still others are written and printed by individual brokers. When selling or buying, get a copy of the earnest money agreement form that the broker uses. Read every word of it. It is usually in simple language. Ask questions of the salesperson. Consult your attorney.

All forms should cover these subjects just in case you, as a buyer, ever want to specifically enforce your contract.

(a) A description of the property — *legal* and residential
(b) The names of the buyers
(c) The agreement to sell and buy
(d) The price
(e) The amount of earnest money
(f) The down payment
(g) The balance and means of payment
(h) The title term (see chapter 7)
(i) Title insurance provisions (see chapter 6)
(j) What happens if the earnest money is forfeited
(k) Date of transfer of possession
(l) Escrow provisions

But a form is just that, and every transaction is individual. It is up to the parties, both buyer and seller, to see that it becomes tailor-made by adding or subtracting from it.

Some real estate brokers prepare a debit and credit form for the buyer and seller (see Sample #5). On it are listed all of the approximate proceeds and expenses that each is going to incur in the transaction. It shows with reasonable accuracy, for example, how much the seller will expect on the date set for completion and how much the buyer can expect to have ready to transfer to the seller on the completion date.

This is quite useful especially in those deals where a sale is actually dependent upon the completion of one or two prior transactions going through.

SAMPLE #3
EARNEST MONEY AGREEMENT

FORM No. 6718 (Escrow).
Stevens-Ness Law Publishing Co. ©
Portland, Oregon 97204   TO

EARNEST MONEY RECEIPT.

City __Portland__ State __Oregon__ , __August 1__ , 19__90__

A. RECEIVED FROM Albert Jones and Ruth Jones, husband and wife,

(hereinafter called "purchaser") the sum of One Thousand and No/100ths------------------------------------Dollars ($ 1,000.00

in the form of __check__   CASH, CHECK, DRAFT   as earnest money and in part payment for the purchase of the following described real estate situated in the City of __Portland__ ,

County of __Multnomah__ , State of __Oregon__ , to-wit:

Lot 5, Block 4, HAZELWOOD TERRACE, commonly known as 5521 S.W. Hazelwood Drive

which we have this day sold to said purchaser

for the sum of Fifty-five Thousand Five Hundred and No/100ths-------------------------Dollars ($ 55,500.00)

on the following terms, to-wit: The sum, hereinabove receipted for, of One Thousand and No/100ths-----------Dollars ($ 1,000.00)
on owner's acceptance. (Strike whichever not applicable)

Upon acceptance of title and delivery of { deed } the sum of (Strike whichever not applicable) Ten Thousand One Hundred Dollars ($ 10,100.00)

Balance of Forty-four Thousand Four Hundred and No/100ths----------------------Dollars ($ 44,400.00)

payable as follows: From the proceeds of an 80% conventional mortgage loan for which purchaser shall apply not later than August 7, 1990 This sale is contingent upon purchaser obtaining the loan.

1) A title insurance policy from a reliable company insuring marketable title in seller is to be furnished purchaser in due course at seller's expense; preliminary to closing, seller may furnish a title insurance company's title report showing its willingness to issue title insurance, which shall be conclusive evidence as to seller's record title.
2) It is agreed that if seller does not approve this sale within the period allowed broker below in which to secure seller's acceptance, or if the title to the said premises is not insurable or marketable, or cannot be made so within thirty days after notice containing a written statement of defects is delivered to seller, the said earnest money shall be refunded. But if said sale is approved by seller and title to the said premises is insurable or marketable and purchaser neglects or refuses to comply with any of said conditions within ten days after the said evidence of title is furnished and to make payments promptly, as hereinabove set forth, then the earnest money herein receipted for (including said additional earnest money) shall be forfeited and disposed of as stated in Section F below and this contract thereupon shall be of no further binding effect.
3) The property is to be conveyed by good and sufficient deed free and clear of all liens and encumbrances except zoning ordinances, building and use restrictions, reservations in Federal

patents, easements of record and.   No exceptions
4) All irrigation, plumbing and heating fixtures and equipment (including stoker and oil tanks but excluding fireplace fixtures and equipment), water heaters, electric light fixtures, light bulbs and fluorescent lamps, bathroom fixtures, venetian blinds, drapery and curtain rods, window and door screens, storm doors and windows, attached linoleum, attached television antenna, all shrubs and trees and all fixtures except   None

are to be left upon the premises as part of the property purchased. The following personal property is also included as a part of the property for said purchase price: None

5) Seller and purchaser agree to pro rate the taxes which are due and payable for the current tax year. Rents, interest, premiums for existing insurance and other matters shall be pro rated on a calendar year basis. Adjustments are to be made as of the date of the consummation at said sale or delivery of possession, whichever first occurs. Encumbrances to be discharged by seller may be paid at his option out of purchase money at date of closing. SELLER AND PURCHASER AGREE THAT SUBJECT SALE WILL BE CLOSED IN ESCROW, THE COST OF WHICH SHALL BE BORNE CO-EQUALLY BETWEEN SELLER AND PURCHASER.
6) Possession of said premises is to be delivered to purchaser on or before __October 1__, 19 __90__, or as soon thereafter as existing laws and regulations will permit removal of tenants, if any. Time is the essence of this contract. This contract is binding upon the heirs, executors, administrators, successors and assigns of buyer and seller. However, the purchaser's rights herein are not assignable without written consent of seller. In any suit or action brought on this contract, the losing party herein agrees to pay the prevailing party herein (1) the prevailing party's reasonable attorney's fees in such suit or action, to be fixed by the trial court, and (2) on appeal if any, similar fees on the appellate court, to be fixed by the appellate court.

Address __321 S.E. Quicksale__   __Quicksale Realty__   □ Cooperating Broker ☒ Listing Broker

Phone __791-2210__   By __J. Quicksale__

B.   **AGREEMENT TO PURCHASE**

I hereby agree to purchase and pay the price of $ __55,500.00__ to purchase the property herein described in its present condition, as set forth above and grant to said agent

a period of __2__ days hereafter to secure seller's acceptance hereof, during which period my offer shall not be subject to revocation. Said deed or contract to be in the name

of __Albert Jones and Ruth Jones, husband and wife__

Address __1212 S.E. Wood Street, Portland, Oregon__   __Albert Jones__   Purchaser

Phone __781-2912__   __Ruth Jones__   Purchaser

C.   **BUYER'S AND SELLER'S AGREEMENT RE DEPOSIT OF EARNEST MONEY**   __August 1__   , 19 __90__

The Earnest Money deposit in this transaction of $ __500.00__ in the form stated above shall be deposited in the Client's Trust Account of the Broker indicated above, until this offer

is accepted, whereupon the parties agree and direct that such funds be deposited in escrow with __Lawyers Title Insurance Co.__

Address __10761 S.E. 76th Avenue, Portland, Oregon__

to be held pending closing of this transaction pursuant to the attached escrow instructions.

__Albert Jones__   Purchaser   __Joseph Seller__   Seller

__Ruth Jones__   Purchaser   __Irene Seller__   Seller

D.   **AGREEMENT TO SELL**   __August 2,__   , 19 __90__

I hereby approve and accept the above sale for said price and on said terms and conditions and agree to consummate the same as stated.

Seller's Address __5521 S.W. Hazelwood Drive, Portland, Oregon__   __Joseph Seller__   Seller

Phone __781-3721__   __Irene Seller__   Seller

E. Deliver promptly to purchaser, either manually or by registered mail, a copy hereof showing seller's acceptance.
Buyer acknowledges receipt of the foregoing instrument bearing his signature and that of the seller   Copy hereof showing seller's signed acceptance sent buyer by registered mail to
showing acceptance.   __Albert Jones__ Purchaser   buyer's above address
                                (return receipt requested) on _____ , 19 ___
Date __August 2, 90__   __Ruth Jones__ Purchaser   Return receipt card received   __Not Applicable__ , 19 ___
                                and attached to broker's copy

F.   **SELLER'S CLOSING INSTRUCTIONS AND AGREEMENT WITH BROKER RE FORFEITED EARNEST MONEY**   __August 2__   19 __90__

I, the seller whose signature appears below, agree to pay forthwith to said broker a commission amounting to $ __3,885.00__ for services rendered in this transaction. In the event that the buyer's deposit is forfeited pursuant to sub-paragraph 2, above, said forfeited deposit shall be disposed of between broker and seller in the following manner:

half to seller; half to broker

Seller acknowledges receipt of a copy of this contract bearing signatures of seller and buyer named above.

__Quicksale Realty__   Broker   __Joseph Seller__   __Joseph Seller__   Seller

By __J. Quicksale__   __J. Quicksale__   __Irene Seller__   __Irene Seller__   Seller

BROKER'S COPY   FILE IN DEAL ENVELOPE

NOTE: IF ANY BLANK SPACES ARE INSUFFICIENT, USE S-N No. 810
"HANDY PAD", TO BE SEPARATELY SIGNED BY BUYER AND SELLER.

784

SAMPLE #4
SEVENTY-TWO HOUR CONTINGENCY SALE

SEVENTY-TWO HOUR CONTINGENCY SALE

ADDENDUM TO EARNEST MONEY RECEIPT AND AGREEMENT TO

PURCHASE CONTINGENT UPON SALE OF PURCHASERS' HOME

THIS ADDENDUM IS A PART OF THAT CERTAIN EARNEST MONEY RECEIPT AND CONTRACT, dated ___September 30___ , 19 __90__ , between

___Sally & Sol Homeowner___ , Seller(s) and

___Ruth & Albert Jones___ , Purchaser(s).

Said Counter Offer to Earnest Money Agreement in the amount of $ __60,000__ , is expressly conditioned and contingent upon the sale of purchaser's home, located at ___123 Purchaser Street___ , (city) __Portland__ , Oregon, within ___30___ days of seller's execution of said Earnest Money Agreement.

It is further agreed and understood that seller reserves the right to keep __Lot 5, Block 4, Hazelwood Terrace__ on the market for sale. In the event that, prior to purchaser selling the above mentioned home, or expiration of the above mentioned time limit, the Seller received another acceptable written offer to purchase, the seller shall give written notice of the receipt thereof to purchaser and to the agent. Thereupon the purchaser shall have a period of seventy-two (72) hours from receipt of said notice within which to deliver to the seller and the agent a waiver of the above condition and contingency. Both parties shall thereupon proceed to close this sale as expeditiously as possible.

In the event that the purchaser does not so waive said condition and contingency, then this Earnest Money Agreement shall be null and void, all rights of the parties hereto shall cease and terminate, and the Earnest Money shall be returned in its entirety, to the purchaser forthwith.

Sally Homeowner _Sally Homeowner_	Ruth Jones _Ruth Jones_
SELLER	PURCHASER
Sol Homeowner _Sol Homeowner_	Albert Jones _Albert Jones_
SELLER	PURCHASER
DATE: __October 1/90__	DATE: __October 1/90__

Original: Broker
1st Copy: Seller
2nd Copy: Purchaser

24

d. WARRANTIES

One warning about some of the earnest money agreements commonly in use in Oregon today: these contain a clause in which the seller gives a limited warranty that the heating, plumbing and electrical systems are in working order. Before signing, consider carefully whether these warranties are appropriate. What about the age of this equipment? Since much of it is behind the walls or under cover is it really in good working order?

The law in this area is still developing. For many years a person who bought a defective house, without any express warranty, had no recourse. You had to pay for the repairs yourself. Now, warranty against defects comes up in several ways:

1. Implied warranty

In 1974 the Supreme Court of Oregon ruled that the sale of a new residence by a builder carried with it an implied warranty against defects. This implied warranty is very limited. It applies *only* to residences sold by a builder. It does not apply to used housing or to commercial structures.

The Oregon court has indicated that it is not going to be liberal with the doctrine of implied warranty because it has refused to extend it to bare land to be used for a residence or to a house built on the owner's lot — reasoning that buyers of lots and owners of custom built houses can protect themselves by making inspections, unlike the buyer of a completed dwelling.

2. Warranty contracts

Various warranty contracts are now available through certain realtors and builders. These cover defects in the structures, used or new. They are desirable. Part of your negotiations should include this subject and who, seller or buyer, is to pay for the warranty contract.

SAMPLE #5
CREDIT AND DEBIT FORM FOR
BUYERS AND SELLERS

Ramada Realty
Mel Fox, Broker
256-011

R
REALTOR®

SELLER'S ESTIMATED CREDIT & DEBIT FORM

SELLER: _____ Sol Homeowner _____

PROPERTY ADDRESS: _111 Movin Lane, Portland_

ESTIMATED CLOSING DATE: _3-4 weeks_

SELLER'S ESTIMATED CREDITS

Sales Price	$ 55,700.00
Reserve Account & ins.	951.60
Tax Pro-Rates (Nov. 1 to June 30)	
Appraisal Fee.....................	
Insurance Pro-Rates	
Oil in fuel tank (Direct from buyer) ...	

TOTAL ESTIMATED CREDITS $ 56,651.60

SELLER'S ESTIMATED DEBITS

Realtor Brokerage Fee	$ 3899.00
Title Insurance Policy	238.00
Escrow Fee (one-half)	114.00
Guarantee Sales Fee	
Mortgage Discount to Lender........	
Drafting of Contract................	
Attorney Fees.....................	
Existing Mortgage Balance (Approx.)	8760.37
Second Mortgage..................	
Interest to Closing Date	76.66
Pay-Off Penalty	
Recording of Satisfaction	18.50
Required Repairs	
Home Improvement Loan (if any)	
Property Taxes (July 1 to Oct. 30)	386.28 7/1–10/25
City or County Inspection Fees	
City or County Liens	
Delinquent Taxes..................	
Judgements	
Credit to Purchaser	
Final Water Bill	15.00
Other _Oil direct from purchaser_	

TOTAL ESTIMATED DEBITS $ 13,507.81

APPROXIMATE NET PROCEEDS ...$ 43,143.79

The undersigned seller hereby acknowledges receipt of a copy of this _estimate._

Initial _____ Submitted by: _____

This transaction will be closed in escrow and final closing procedures and figures are the responsibility of the escrow agent — not the Realtor — these figures are _estimates_ only and not guaranteed to be complete or accurate.

PORTLAND, OREGON 97216

256-0111

26

Ramada Realty

Mel Fox, Broker
MOVE IN COST ESTIMATE

PURCHASER: Paula Purchaser
PROPERTY ADDRESS: 111 Movin Lane , Portland
TYPE OF FINANCING: 80% Co nventional
ESTIMATED PROCESSING TIME: 3-4 weeks

Sales Price .... $ 55,700
Mortgage Loan/Contract Balance .. $ 44,550
Down Payment .... $ 11,150

LOAN COSTS AND FEES: Estimated
Loan Fee .... $ 670.00
Insured Loan Insurance Fee .... $
Assumption Fee .... $
Contract Prep Fee .... $
Credit Report .... $ 30.00
Survey .... $ 35.00
Picture......................... $ 10.00
Tax Service Fee .... $ 17.00
F.H.A. or an Appraisal Fee .... $ 50.00
Recording Fee .... $ 15.00
Escrow Fee (one-half) .... $ 115.00
Prepaid Interest .... $ 280.00
Mortgagee's Title Ins. ALTA ...... $ 110.00

TOTAL ESTIMATED COSTS:................ $ 1335.00

RESERVES & PRO-RATES: Estimated
Property Tax (10 Mo.)............ $ 740.00
Fire Ins. (12 Mo.)................ $ 168.00
One month F.H.A. Ins............ $

TOTAL ESTIMATED RESERVES: .... $ 908.00

TOTAL ESTIMATED CASH OUTLAY: .... $ 13,393.00

MONTHLY PAYMENT ESTIMATE

For 30 Years
Rate of Interest 11¼ % (approx.)
Principal, Interest & Loan Ins...... $ 429.00
Tax Reserves .... $ 74.00
Insurance Reserves .... $ 14.00

APPROXIMATE TOTAL MONTHLY PAYMENT $ 517.00
Buyer agrees to pay for oil in tank Direct to Seller. YES

The undersigned purchaser hereby acknowledges receipt of a copy
of this estimate:
Signature _____ Submitted by: _____

Portland, Oregon 97233   **256-0111**

3. Express warranties

Some builders expressly warrant their product against defects. This is essentially a matter of contract terms. But any contract is only as good as the person who is to perform it.

4. Negligence

The Oregon Supreme Court has ruled that a subdivider could be held liable to a buyer for negligence in the development of a subdivision. The law on this subject is still developing. In future cases, the rule may be extended to negligent building construction.

5
HOW TO PAY FOR YOUR HOUSE

Mortgages, deeds of trust, contracts, and promissory notes contain intricate terms. Unfortunately, most people do not see these documents until the closing of the sale when the atmosphere is not conducive to careful study. Try to obtain advance copies of all documents you will be asked to sign, so you can study them at leisure, and consult your advisers. More will be discussed about financing in the chapter on foreclosures (see chapter 11).

Most buyers will want to make the purchase contingent upon obtaining a loan to pay for the property. The seller, being fully paid, deeds the property to the buyer, who in turn gives it to the lender as collateral for the loan. There are many kinds of financing — commercial, governmental, and private. Essentially, financing the sale can take any one of these shapes:

(a) Mortgage

(b) Deed of Trust

(c) Contract of Sale

(d) Assumption of existing debt

Which is best? If you borrow from a professional lender (bank, mortgage company, etc.) it does not matter, because you will either use the method and form it provides or not get the loan. But in the privately financed sale, you can negotiate.

a. PRIVATE FINANCING
1. Mortgage
In a sale on mortgage (see Sample #6), the seller transfers the property to the buyer who immediately gives the seller a mortgage on it as a collateral for the money owing, which

usually is in the form of a note. In effect, the property is pledged for the debt. As a general rule, you should never sell to a buyer who wants you to take a mortgage back because there are better ways! And, too, you usually want to get your money out so you can buy another home.

2. Deed of trust

In this situation, the seller transfers the property by way of deed to the buyer who then gives it up to a trustee who holds title for the benefit of the creditor (either a lender or the seller) until the debt is paid; the trustee then conveys the property by way of deed to the buyer. A deed of trust has the advantage that it can be foreclosed outside of court unlike a conventional mortgage. (See Sample #7.)

Only the following who are authorized to do business in Oregon can act as trustee: an attorney at law, a bank or savings and loan association, a title insurance company, the United States or any agency thereof, an escrow agent.

3. Contract of sale

The seller keeps the deed and title to the property, but contracts to deliver these to the buyer when all installment payments due under the contract are made. When the contract is fully paid, the seller then transfers the property to the buyer. Until this happens the buyer has equity possession (possession by right of law rather than clear title) and all other incidents of ownership (see Sample #8).

In most circumstances it is safe to use a contract of sale to purchase property. In fact, it has great advantages because the buyer's closing costs are minimal. But be careful. You are on your own for the most part. Almost all contract sales are by private sellers. Therefore, you will not have the protection given you by a commercial lender who has the same concerns about getting a good mortgage as you do about getting a good title and thus will carry out all the necessary steps in a proper investigation of the state of the title, etc. This is one place where the services of a lawyer can be invaluable. Other real estate professionals, such as title examiners, real estate salespersons, and

SAMPLE #6
MORTGAGE

FORM No. 105A—MORTGAGE—One Page Long Form

SN

THIS MORTGAGE, Made this 30th **day of** September , 19 90 ,
by Bruce Buyer and Sally Buyer, husband and wife

Mortgagor,

to Sam Seller and Betty Seller, husband and wife

Mortgagee,

WITNESSETH, That said mortgagor, in consideration of Forty Thousand and 00/00
(40,000.00)- Dollars, to him paid by said mortgagee, does hereby grant, bargain, sell and convey unto said mortgagee, his heirs, executors, administrators and assigns, that certain real property situated in Multnomah County, State of Oregon, bounded and described as follows, to-wit:

Lot 8, Block 10, GREEN TREES, in the City of Portland, County of Multnomah and State of Oregon

Together with all and singular the tenements, hereditaments and appurtenances thereunto belonging or in anywise appertaining, and which may hereafter thereto belong or appertain, and the rents, issues and profits therefrom, and any and all fixtures upon said premises at the time of the execution of this mortgage or at any time during the term of this mortgage.

TO HAVE AND TO HOLD the said premises with the appurtenances unto the said mortgagee, his heirs, executors, administrators and assigns forever.

This mortgage is intended to secure the payment of One *promissory note , of which the following is a substantial copy:*

$ 40,000.00 Portland, Oregon , September 30 , 19 90
I (or if more than one maker) we, jointly and severally, promise to pay to the order of
Sam Seller and Betty Seller
at Portland, Oregon
Forty Thousand and 00/100 ($40,000.00)- DOLLARS,
with interest thereon at the rate of 10 percent per annum from until paid, payable in
monthly installments of not less than $ 435.00 in any one payment; interest shall be paid monthly and
※ ⓧⓧⓧⓧⓧⓧⓧⓧ the minimum payments above required; the first payment to be made on the first day of November .
19 90 , and a like payment on the first day of each month thereafter, until the whole sum, principal and interest has been paid; if any of said installments is not so paid, all principal and interest to become immediately due and collectible at the option of the holder of this note. If this note is placed in the hands of an attorney for collection, I/we promise and agree to pay holder's reasonable attorney's fees and collection costs, even though no suit or action is filed hereon; however, if a suit or an action is filed, the amount of such reasonable attorney's fees shall be fixed by the court, or courts in which the suit or action, including any appeal therein, is tried, heard or decided.
* Strike words not applicable.

Bruce Buyer *Bruce Buyer*
Sally Buyer *Sally Buyer*

FORM No. 217—INSTALLMENT NOTE. SN Stevens-Ness Law Publishing Co., Portland, Ore.

And said mortgagor covenants to and with the mortgagee, his heirs, executors, administrators and assigns, that he is lawfully seized in fee simple of said premises and has a valid, unencumbered title thereto

and will warrant and forever defend the same against all persons; that he will pay said note, principal and interest, according to the terms thereof; that while any part of said note remains unpaid he will pay all taxes, assessments and other charges of every nature which may be levied or assessed against said property, or this mortgage or the note above described, when due and payable and before the same may become delinquent; that he will promptly pay and satisfy any and all liens or encumbrances that are or may become liens on the premises or any part thereof superior to the lien of this mortgage; that he will keep the buildings now on or which hereafter may be erected on the said premises continuously insured against loss or damage by fire and such other hazards as the mortgagee may from time to time require, in an amount not less than the original principal sum of the note or obligation secured by this mortgage, in a company or companies acceptable to the mortgagee, with loss payable first to the mortgagee and then to the mortgagor as their respective interests may appear; all policies of insurance shall be delivered to the mortgagee as soon as insured. Now if the mortgagor shall fail for any reason to procure any such insurance and to deliver said policies to the mortgagee at least fifteen days prior to the expiration of any policy of insurance now or hereafter placed on said buildings, the mortgagee may procure the same at mortgagor's expense; that he will keep the buildings and improvements on said premises in good repair and will not commit or suffer any waste of said premises. At the request of the mortgagee, the mortgagor shall join with the mortgagee in executing one or more financing statements pursuant to the Uniform Commercial Code, in form satisfactory to the mortgagee, and will pay for filing the same in the proper public office or offices, as well as the cost of all lien searches made by filing officers or searching agencies as may be deemed desirable by the mortgagee.

SAMPLE #6 — Continued

The mortgagor warrants that the proceeds of the loan represented by the above described note and this mortgage are: (a)* primarily for mortgagor's personal, family, household or agricultural purposes (see Important Notice below), (XXXXX XX XXXXXXXXXX XXXXXX XXXXXXXX XX XXXXXX XXXXXX XXX XX XXXXXX XX XXXXXXXX XXXXXXX XXX XXX agricultural purposes.

Now, therefore, if said mortgagor shall keep and perform the covenants herein contained and shall pay said note according to its terms, this conveyance shall be void, but otherwise shall remain in full force as a mortgage to secure the performance of all of said covenants and the payment of said note; it being agreed that a failure to perform any covenant herein, or if a proceeding of any kind be taken to foreclose any lien on said premises or any part thereof, the mortgagee shall have the option to declare the whole amount unpaid on said note or on this mortgage at once due and payable, and this mortgage may be foreclosed at any time thereafter. And if the mortgagor shall fail to pay any taxes or charges or any lien, encumbrance or insurance premium as above provided for, the mortgagee may at his option do so, and any payment so made shall be added to and become a part of the debt secured by this mortgage, and shall bear interest at the same rate as said note without waiver, however, of any right arising to the mortgagee for breach of covenant. And this mortgage may be foreclosed for principal, interest and all sums paid by the mortgagee at any time while the mortgagor neglects to repay any sums so paid by the mortgagee. In the event of any suit or action being instituted to foreclose this mortgage, the mortgagor agrees to pay all reasonable costs incurred by the mortgagee for title reports and title search, all statutory costs and disbursements and such further sum as the trial court may adjudge reasonable as plaintiff's attorney's fees in such suit or action, and if an appeal is taken from any judgment or decree entered therein mortgagor further promises to pay such sum as the appellate court shall adjudge reasonable as plaintiff's attorney's fees on such appeal, all sums to be secured by the lien of this mortgage and included in the decree of foreclosure.

Each and all of the covenants and agreements herein contained shall apply to and bind the heirs, executors, administrators and assigns of said mortgagor and of said mortgagee respectively.

In case suit or action is commenced to foreclose this mortgage, the Court, may upon motion of the mortgagee, appoint a receiver to collect the rents and profits arising out of said premises during the pendency of such foreclosure, and apply the same, after first deducting all of said receiver's proper charges and expenses, to the payment of the amount due under this mortgage.

In construing this mortgage, it is understood that the mortgagor or mortgagee may be more than one person; that if the context so requires, the singular pronoun shall be taken to mean and include the plural, the masculine, the feminine and the neuter, and that generally all grammatical changes shall be made, assumed and implied to make the provisions hereof apply equally to corporations and to individuals.

IN WITNESS WHEREOF, said mortgagor has hereunto set his hand the day and year first above written.

Bruce Buyer

Sally Buyer

*IMPORTANT NOTICE: Delete, by lining out, whichever warranty (a) or (b) is not applicable; if warranty (a) is applicable and if the mortgagee is a creditor, as such word is defined in the Truth-in-Lending Act and Regulation Z, the mortgagee MUST comply with the Act and Regulation by making required disclosures; for this purpose, if this instrument is to be a FIRST lien to finance the purchase of a dwelling, use Stevens-Ness Form No. 1305 or equivalent; if this instrument is NOT to be a first lien, use Stevens-Ness Form No. 1306, or equivalent.

MORTGAGE (FORM No. 1861)

Bruce Buyer and Sally Buyer

TO

Sam Seller and Betty Seller

STATE OF OREGON,
County of Multnomah } ss.

I certify that the within instrument was received for record on the 1st day of October, 1990, at 10:00 o'clock A.M., and recorded in book 1521 on page 321 or as filing fee number

Record of Mortgages of said County.

Witness my hand and seal of County affixed.

Robert L. Daily
Recorder

By Carrie Montgomery
Deputy.

Title.

STEVENS-NESS LAW PUB. CO., PORTLAND, ORE.

Sam Seller and Betty Seller
3658 Southeast 176th Avenue
Portland, Oregon 97233

STATE OF OREGON,
County of Multnomah } ss.

BE IT REMEMBERED, That on this 30th day of September , 1990 , before me, the undersigned, a notary public in and for said county and state, personally appeared the within named Bruce Buyer and Sally Buyer, husband and wife

known to me to be the identical individual s described in and who executed the within instrument and acknowledged to me that they executed the same freely and voluntarily.

IN TESTIMONY WHEREOF, I have hereunto set my hand and affixed my official seal the day and year last above written.

Thomas C. Sojac
Notary Public for Oregon.
My Commission expires Nov. 7/92

32

escrow officers, will also assist you. You should be aware, however, that these people, while competent, are not lawyers and the interests they serve are not identical with your own.

A large percentage (perhaps the majority) of contract sales are made by a seller who owns an existing mortgage, deed of trust, or contract, and who will continue to do so even after selling. Is this safe for a buyer? Yes, if you protect yourself. It is essential that your monthly payment totally controls the transaction so that you do not find yourself in the unhappy position of having made all of your payments on time to a seller who has defaulted in his or her own mortgage or other debt instrument, and whose creditors are now foreclosing to take the property from both the seller and you. My own experience suggests this doesn't happen very often but since there is no way of knowing in advance what will happen, take precautions in drawing up the contract of sale. The procedure is comparatively simple. Insist that your monthly payment be made directly into a mandatory collection account which first pays the seller's debt and then pays the surplus to him or her.

In the Portland metropolitan area the usual procedure is to sign only a contract of sale. However, in the rest of Oregon, these additional things are done. A deed is signed simultaneously with the contract. The seller deposits the deed with a bank to which the buyer makes all payments. When the contract is fully paid, the bank then delivers the deed to the buyer. This excellent method is also available in Portland but seldom recognized or recommended.

From a seller's point of view, a properly drafted real estate contract is highly desirable. Because of recent developments in Oregon law it gives the seller the best of all worlds.

To enforce a contract a seller has a wide range of remedies. The seller can sue to foreclose, sue for specific performance, sue for the debt, or maintain non-judicial proceedings to cause forfeiture of the buyer's equity. These will be discussed in the chapter on foreclosure.

SAMPLE #7
DEED OF TRUST

STATE OF OREGON
FHA FORM NO. 2160t
Rev. April 1971

DEED OF TRUST

* THIS DEED OF TRUST, made this __15th__ day of __September__ , 19__90__,

between __Albert Jones and Ruth Jones, husband and wife,__

_____ , as grantor,

whose address is __1509 Pearl Street__ __Eugene__ State of Oregon,
(Street and number)   (City)

__Safeco Title Insurance Company,__ , as Trustee, and

__Lotsamoney Bank,__ , as Beneficiary.

WITNESSETH: That Grantor irrevocably GRANTS, BARGAINS, SELLS and CONVEYS to TRUSTEE IN TRUST, WITH

POWER OF SALE, THE PROPERTY IN _____ __Multnomah__ ____ County, State of Oregon, described as:

Lot 5, Block 4, HAZELWOOD TERRACE, in the City of Portland, County of
Multnomah, State of Oregon.

Together with all the tenements, hereditaments, and appurtenances now or hereafter thereunto belonging or in anywise appertaining, the rents, issues, and profits thereof, SUBJECT, HOWEVER, to the right, power, and authority hereinafter given to and conferred upon Beneficiary to collect and apply such rents, issues, and profits.

TO HAVE AND TO HOLD the same, with the appurtenances, unto Trustee. The above described property does not exceed three acres.

FOR THE PURPOSE OF SECURING PERFORMANCE of each agreement of Grantor herein contained and payment of the sum

** of $ __22,000.00__ with interest thereon according to the terms of a promissory note, dated __September 15,__

___, 19 __85__, payable to Beneficiary or order and made by Grantor, the final payment of principal and interest thereof, if not sooner paid, shall be due and payable on the first day of _____ __October__ ____ __2015__

1. Privilege is reserved to pay the debt in whole, or in an amount equal to one or more monthly payments on the principal that are next due on the note, on the first day of any month prior to maturity: *Provided, however,* That written notice on an intention to exercise such privilege is given at least thirty (30) days prior to prepayment; *and provided further,* That in the event this debt is paid in full prior to maturity and at that time it is insured under the provisions of the National Housing Act, all parties liable for the payment of same, whether principal, surety, guarantor or endorser, agree to be jointly and severally bound to pay to the holder of the note secured hereby an adjusted premium charge of one per centum (1%) of the original principal amount thereof, except that in no event shall the adjusted premium exceed the aggregate amount of premium charges which would have been payable if this Deed of Trust and the note secured hereby had continued to be insured until maturity; such payment to be applied by the holder thereof upon its obligation to the Secretary of Housing and Urban Development on account of mortgage insurance.

2. Grantor agrees to pay to Beneficiary in addition to the monthly payments of principal and interest payable under the terms of said note, on the first day of each month until said note is fully paid, the following sums:

(a) An amount sufficient to provide the holder hereof with funds to pay the next mortgage insurance premium if this instrument and the note secured hereby are insured, or a monthly charge (in lieu of a mortgage insurance premium) if they are held by the Secretary of Housing and Urban Development as follows:

(I) If and so long as said note of even date and this instrument are insured or are reinsured under the provisions of the National Housing Act, an amount sufficient to accumulate in the hands of the holder one (1) month prior to its due date the annual mortgage insurance premium, in order to provide such holder with funds to pay such premium to the Secretary of Housing and Urban Development pursuant to the National Housing Act, as amended, and applicable Regulations thereunder; or

(II) If and so long as said note of even date and this instrument are held by the Secretary of Housing and Urban Development, a monthly charge (in lieu of a mortgage insurance premium) which shall be in an amount equal to one-twelfth (1/12) of one-half (1/2) per centum of the average outstanding balance due on the note computed without taking into account delinquencies or prepayments;

(b) A sum, as estimated by the Beneficiary, equal to the ground rents, if any, and the taxes and special assessments next due on the premises covered by this Deed of Trust, plus the premiums that will next become due and payable on policies of fire and other hazard insurance on the premises covered hereby as may be required by Beneficiary in amounts and in a company or companies satisfactory to Beneficiary, Grantor agreeing to deliver promptly to Beneficiary all bills and notices therefor, less all sums already paid therefor divided by the number of months to elapse before 1 month prior to the date when such ground rents, premiums, taxes and assessments will become delinquent, such sums to be held by the Beneficiary in trust to pay said ground rents, premiums, taxes and special assessments, before the same become delinquent; and

(c) All payments mentioned in the two preceding subsections of this paragraph and all payments to be made under the note secured hereby shall be added together and the aggregate amount thereof shall be paid each month in a single payment to be applied by Beneficiary to the following items in the order set forth:

(I) premium charges under the contract of insurance with the Secretary of Housing and Urban Development, or monthly charge (in lieu of mortgage insurance premium), as the case may be;

(II) ground rents, if any, taxes, special assessments, fire and other hazard insurance premiums;

*A purchaser could sign and file one of these to record a buyer's interest (as beneficiary) under a contract of sale.

**The prepayment terms are set out here.

34

(III) interest on the note secured hereby; and
(IV) amortization of the principal of the said note.

Any deficiency in the amount of any such aggregate monthly payment shall, unless made good prior to the due date of the next such payment, constitute an event of default under this Deed of Trust.

3. In the event that any payment or portion thereof is not paid within fifteen (15) days from the date the same is due, Grantor agrees to pay a "late charge" of two cents (2¢) for each dollar so overdue, if charged by Beneficiary.

4. If the total of the payments made by Grantor under (b) of paragraph 2 preceding shall exceed the amount of payments actually made by Beneficiary for ground rents, taxes or assessments, or insurance premiums, as the case may be, such excess, at the option of Beneficiary, shall be credited by Beneficiary on subsequent payments to be made by Grantor, or refunded to Grantor. If, however, the monthly payments made under (b) of paragraph 2 preceding shall not be sufficient to pay ground rents, taxes, and assessments, and insurance premiums, as the case may be, when the same shall become due and payable, then Grantor shall pay to Beneficiary any amount necessary to make up the deficiency on or before the date when payment of such ground rents, taxes, assessments, or insurance premiums shall be due. If at any time Grantor shall tender to Beneficiary, in accordance with the provisions hereof, full payment of the entire indebtedness secured hereby, Beneficiary shall, in computing the amount of indebtedness, credit to the account of Grantor all payments made under the provisions of (a) of paragraph 2, which the Beneficiary has not become obligated to pay to the Secretary of Housing and Urban Development, and any balance remaining in the funds accumulated under the provisions of (b) of paragraph 2 hereof. If there shall be a default under any of the provisions of this Deed of Trust and thereafter a sale of the premises in accordance with the provisions hereof, or if the Beneficiary acquires the property otherwise after default, Beneficiary shall apply, at the time of the commencement of such proceedings, or at the time the property is otherwise acquired, the balance then remaining in the funds accumulated under (b) of paragraph 2 preceding, as a credit against the amount of principal then remaining unpaid under said note and shall properly adjust any payments which shall have been made under (a) of paragraph 2.

TO PROTECT THE SECURITY OF THIS DEED OF TRUST, GRANTOR AGREES:

5. To keep said premises in as good order and condition as they now are and not to commit or permit any waste thereof, reasonable wear and tear excepted.

6. To complete or restore promptly and in good workmanlike manner any building or improvement which may be constructed, damaged, or destroyed thereon, and pay when due all costs incurred therefor, and, if the loan secured hereby or any part thereof is being obtained for the purpose of financing construction of improvements on said property, Grantor further agrees:

(a) to commence construction promptly and in any event within 30 days from the date of the commitment of the Department of Housing and Urban Development, and complete same in accordance with plans and specifications satisfactory to Beneficiary,
(b) to allow Beneficiary to inspect said property at all times during construction,
(c) to replace any work or materials unsatisfactory to Beneficiary, within fifteen (15) calendar days after written notice from Beneficiary of such fact, which notice may be given to the Grantor by registered mail, sent to his last known address, or by personal service of the same,
(d) that work shall not cease on the construction of such improvements for any reason whatsoever for a period of fifteen (15) calendar days.

The Trustee, upon presentation to it of an affidavit signed by Beneficiary, setting forth facts showing a default by Grantor under this numbered paragraph, is authorized to accept as true and conclusive all facts and statements therein, and to act thereon hereunder.

7. Not to remove or demolish any building or improvement thereon.

8. To comply with all laws, ordinances, regulations, convenants, conditions, and restrictions affecting said property.

9. To provide and maintain insurance against loss by fire and other hazards, casualties, and contingencies including war damage as may be required from time to time by the Beneficiary in such amounts and for such periods as may be required by the Beneficiary, with loss payable to the Beneficiary and Grantor, as their interests may appear, and to deliver all policies to Beneficiary, which delivery shall constitute an assignment to Beneficiary of all return premiums.

10. To appear in and defend any action or proceeding purporting to affect the security hereof or the rights or powers of Beneficiary or Trustee; and should Beneficiary or Trustee elect to also appear in or defend any such action or proceeding, to pay all costs and expenses, including cost of evidence of title and attorney's fees in a reasonable sum incurred by Beneficiary or Trustee.

11. To pay at least 10 days before delinquency all assessments upon water company stock, and all rents, assessments and charges for water, appurtenant to or used in connection with said property; to pay, when due, all encumbrances, charges, and liens with interest, on said property or any part thereof, which at any time appear to be prior or superior hereto; to pay all costs, fees, and expenses of this Trust. If after notice of default, the Grantor prior to trustee's sale pays the entire amount then due, to pay in addition thereto, all costs and expenses actually incurred, and trustee's and attorney's fees actually incurred, not exceeding $50.00.

12. To pay immediately and without demand all sums expended hereunder by Beneficiary or Trustee, with interest from date of expenditure at the rate provided on the principal debt, and the repayment thereof shall be secured hereby.

13. To do all acts and make all payments required of Grantor and of the owner of the property to make said note and this Deed eligible for insurance by Beneficiary under the provisions of the National Housing Act and amendments thereto, and agrees not to do, or cause or suffer to be done, any act which will void such insurance during the existence of this Deed.

IT IS MUTUALLY AGREED THAT:

14. Should Grantor fail to make any payment or to do any act as herein provided, then Beneficiary or Trustee, but without obligation so to do and without notice to or demand upon Grantor and without releasing Grantor from any obligation hereof, may: Make or do the same in such manner and to such extent as either may deem necessary to protect the security hereof, Beneficiary or Trustee being authorized to enter upon the property for such purposes; commence, appear in and defend any action or proceeding purporting to affect the security hereof or the rights or powers of Beneficiary or Trustee; pay, purchase, contest, or compromise any encumbrance, charge, or lien which in the judgment of either appears to be prior or superior hereto; and in exercising any such powers, incur any liability, expend whatever amounts in its absolute discretion it may deem necessary therefor, including costs of evidence of title, employ counsel, and pay his reasonable fees.

15. Should the property or any part thereof be taken or damaged by reason of any public improvement or condemnation proceeding, or damaged by fire, or earthquake, or in any other manner, Beneficiary shall be entitled to all compensation, awards, and other payments or relief thereof, and shall be entitled at its option to commence, appear in, and prosecute in its own name, any action or proceedings, or to make any compromise or settlement, in connection with such taking or damage. All such compensation, awards, damages, rights of action and proceeds, including the proceeds of any policies of fire and other insurance affecting said property, are hereby assigned to Beneficiary, who may after deducting therefrom all its expenses, including attorney's fees, release any moneys so received by it or apply the same on any indebtedness secured hereby. Grantor agrees to execute such further assignments of any compensation, award, damage, and rights of action and proceeds as Beneficiary or Trustee may require.

16. By accepting payment of any sum secured hereby after its due date, Beneficiary does not waive its right either to require prompt payment when due of all other sums so secured or to declare default for failure so to pay.

17. At any time and from time to time upon written request of Beneficiary, payment of its fees and presentation of this Deed and the note for endorsement (in case of full reconveyance, for cancellation and retention), without affecting the liability of any person for the payment of the indebtedness Trustee may (a) consent to the making of any map or plat of said property; (b) join in granting any easement or creating any restriction thereon; (c) join in any subordination or other agreement affecting this Deed or the lien of charge thereof; (d) reconvey, without warranty, all or any part of the property.

The Grantee in any reconveyance may be described as the "person or persons legally entitled thereto," and the recitals therein of any matters or facts shall be conclusive proof of the truthfulness thereof.

18. As additional security, Grantor hereby assigns to Beneficiary during the continuance of these trusts, all rents, issues, royalties, and profits of the property affected by this Deed and of any personal property located thereon. Until Grantor shall default in the payment of any indebtedness secured hereby or in the performance of any agreement hereunder, Grantor shall have the right to collect all such rents, issues, royalties, and profits earned prior to default as they become due and payable.

19. Upon any default, Beneficiary may at any time without notice, either in person, by agent, or by a receiver to be appointed by a court, and without regard to the adequacy of any security for the indebtedness hereby secured, enter upon and take possession of said property or any part thereof, in his own name sue for or otherwise collect such rents, issues and profits, including those past due and unpaid, and apply the same, less costs and expenses of operation and collection, including reasonable attorney's fees, upon any indebtedness secured hereby, and in such order as Beneficiary may determine. The entering upon and taking possession of said property, the collection of such rents, issues and profits and the application thereof as aforesaid, shall not cure or waive any default or notice of default hereunder or invalidate any act done pursuant to such notice.

20. Upon default by Grantor in payment of any indebtedness secured hereby or in performance of any agreement hereunder, or should this Deed and said note not be eligible for insurance under the National Housing Act within _____ months from the date hereof (written statement of any officer of the Department of Housing and Urban Development or authorized agent of the Secretary of Housing and Urban Development dated subsequent to _____ months' time from the date of

3

this Deed, declining to insure said note and this Deed, being deemed conclusive proof of such ineligibility), or should the commitment of the Department of Housing and Urban Development to insure this loan cease to be in full force and effect for any reason whatsoever, Beneficiary may declare all sums secured hereby immediately due and payable by delivery to Trustee of written declaration of default and demand for sale, and of written notice of default and of election to cause the property to be sold, which notice Trustee shall cause to be duly filed for record. Beneficiary shall also deposit with Trustee this Deed, the note and all documents evidencing expenditures secured hereby.

21. After the lapse of such time as may then be required by law following the recordation of said notice of default, and notice of sale having been given as then required by law, Trustee, without demand on Grantor, shall sell said property at the time and place fixed by it in said notice of sale, either as a whole or in separate parcels, and in such order as it may determine (but subject to any statutory right of Grantor to direct the order in which such property, if consisting of several known lots or parcels, shall be sold), at public auction to the highest bidder for cash in lawful money of the United States, payable at time of sale. Trustee may postpone sale of all or any portion of said property by public announcement at such time and place of sale, and from time to time thereafter may postpone the sale by public announcement at the time fixed by the preceding postponement. Trustee shall deliver to the purchaser its Deed conveying the property so sold, but without any covenant or warranty, express or implied. The recitals in the Deed of any matters or facts shall be conclusive proof of the truthfulness thereof. Any person, including Grantor, or Beneficiary, may purchase at the sale. After deducting all costs, fees, and expenses of Trustee and of this trust, including cost of title evidence and reasonable attorney's fees, in connection with sale, Trustee shall apply the proceeds of sale to the payment of all sums expended under the terms hereof then repaid, with accrued interest at the rate provided on the principal debt; all other sums then secured hereby; and the remainder, if any, to the person or persons legally entitled thereto.

22. Beneficiary may, from time to time, as provided by statute, appoint another Trustee in place and instead of Trustee herein named, and thereupon the Trustee herein named shall be discharged and Trustee so appointed shall be substituted as Trustee hereunder with the same effect as if originally named Trustee herein.

23. This Deed shall inure to and bind the heirs, legatees, devisees, administrators, executors, successors, and assigns of the parties hereto. All obligations of Grantor hereunder are joint and several. The term "Beneficiary" shall mean the owner and holder, including pledgees, of the note secured hereby, whether or not named as Beneficiary herein.

24. Trustee accepts this Trust when this Deed, duly executed and acknowledged, is made public record as provided by law. Trustee is not obligated to notify any party hereto of pending sale under any other Deed of Trust or of any action or proceeding in which Grantor, Beneficiary, or Trustee shall be a party, unless brought by Trustee.

25. The term "Deed of Trust," as used herein, shall mean the same as, and be synonymous with, the term "Trust Deed," as used in the laws of Oregon relating to Deeds of Trust and Trust Deeds. Whenever used, the singular number shall include the plural, the plural the singular, and the use of any gender shall be applicable to all genders.

Albert Jones _Ruth Jones_
  Signature of Grantor.   _Signature of Grantor._

STATE OF OREGON |
COUNTY OF _____ | ss:

I, the undersigned, ___J. Y. Lawyers_____, hereby certify that on this ____th___ day of ___September___, 19_5_, personally appeared before me __Albert__ ___and Ruth Jones_____
to me known to be the individual described in and who executed the within instrument, and acknowledged that _____.
_____ signed and sealed the same as _____ free and voluntary act and deed, for the uses and purposes therein mentioned.

Given under my hand and official seal the day and year last above written.

___J. Y. Lawyer_____
Notary Public in and for the State of Oregon.

My commission expires _____

REQUEST FOR FULL RECONVEYANCE

Do not record. To be used only when note has been paid.

To: TRUSTEE.
The undersigned is the legal owner and holder of the note and all other indebtedness secured by the within Deed of Trust. Said note, together with all other indebtedness secured by said Deed of Trust, has been fully paid and satisfied; and you are hereby requested and directed on payment to you of any sums owing to you under the terms of said Deed of Trust, to cancel said note above mentioned, and all other evidences of indebtedness secured by said Deed of Trust delivered to you herewith, together with the said Deed of Trust, and to reconvey, without warranty, to the parties designated by the terms of said Deed of Trust, all the estate now held by you thereunder.

Dated _____, 19____   _____

                                   _____

Mail reconveyance to _____

STATE OF OREGON |
COUNTY OF _____ | ss:

I hereby certify that this within Deed of Trust was filed in this office for Record on the _____ day of _____, A.D. 19____, at _____ o'clock ____ M., and was duly recorded in Book _____ of Record of Mortgages of _____ County, State of Oregon, on page _____

                                   _____
                                   Recorder.
                                   By _____
                                   Deputy.

GPO 909-235

36

4. Assumption of existing debt

In this situation, the buyer pays down to the seller's debt balance and takes over all subsequent payments. You must take precautions. Obtain written certification of the balance owing and the current status (i.e., in good standing or in arrears) of the debt you are assuming. This should be signed by the creditor, the person to whom the seller owes the money. Do not rely on anything else. One buyer, who relied on a statement of the balance prepared by the bank collecting the debt he was assuming, ended up in real difficulty. The statement did not reveal that the loan was in default. The Oregon Supreme Court allowed a foreclosure even though the collecting bank was agent of the creditor!

Commercial lenders will generally provide an assumption statement which gives the necessary information. But watch out! Their mortgages and deeds of trust universally contain "due on sale" clauses which in effect allow the lender to declare the full amount payable upon sale of the property. This usually is a device to increase the interest rate at the time of the sale. In effect, the lender says to the new buyer that it will not exercise its legal right to call the debt if the buyer pays higher interest. These provisions are showing up increasingly in private transactions. You should investigate whether your loan is assumable before you sign the earnest money or sales agreement.

Most debt instruments today contain "due on sale" clauses. Even private contracts or mortgages carried by the seller today contain them. You must take care not to be in violation because violation can cause you to suffer a foreclosure on your property. Not all "due on sale" clauses are worded the same and not all of them contain the same restrictions. If in doubt, get professional assistance.

Also note that it is not just the sale of real estate which will activate the "due on sale" clause. Depending on how it is worded, "due on sale" may occur by your granting of an option or a lease with option to purchase or any interest in the real estate, according to one court interpretation.

SAMPLE #8
CONTRACT OF SALE

FORM No. 706—CONTRACT—REAL ESTATE—Monthly Payments.

TT

STEVENS-NESS LAW PUBLISHING CO., PORTLAND, OR. 97204

CONTRACT—REAL ESTATE

THIS CONTRACT, Made this 29th day of September, 19 90, between Sam Seller and Betty Seller, husband and wife

, hereinafter called the seller,

and Bruce Buyer and Sally Buyer, husband and wife

, hereinafter called the buyer,

WITNESSETH: That in consideration of the mutual covenants and agreements herein contained, the seller agrees to sell unto the buyer and the buyer agrees to purchase from the seller all of the following described lands and premises situated in Multnomah County, State of Oregon, to-wit:

Lot 8, Block 10, GREEN TREES, in the City of Portland, County of Multnomah and State of Oregon

for the sum of Fifty Five Thousand and 00/100--------------------Dollars ($ 55,000.00) (hereinafter called the purchase price), on account of which Five Thousand Five Hundred and 00/100 Dollars ($ 5,500.00) is paid on the execution hereof (the receipt of which is hereby acknowledged by the seller); the buyer agrees to pay the remainder of said purchase price (to-wit: $ 49,500.00) to the order of the seller in monthly payments of not less than Four Hundred Thirty Five and 00/100-------- Dollars ($ 435.00) each,

payable on the first day of each month hereafter beginning with the month of November, 19 90, and continuing until said purchase price is fully paid. All of said purchase price may be paid at any time; all deferred balances of said purchase price shall bear interest at the rate of 10 per cent per annum from October 1, 1990 until paid, interest to be paid monthly and * xxxxxxxxxx }being included in the minimum monthly payments above required. Taxes on said premises for the current tax year shall be pro-rated between the parties hereto as of xxxxxxxxxxxxxx October 1, 1990

The buyer warrants to and covenants with the seller that the real property described in this contract is
*(A) primarily for buyer's personal, family, household or agricultural purposes,
(B) xxxxxxxxxxxxxxxxxxxxxxxxxxxxxxxxxxxxxxxxxxxxxxxxxxxxxxxxxxxxxxxxxxxxxxxxxxxxxxxxxxxxxxxxxx

The buyer shall be entitled to possession of said lands on October 1, 19 90, and may retain such possession so long as he is not in default under the terms of this contract. The buyer agrees that at all times he will keep the buildings on said premises, now or hereafter erected, in good condition and repair and will not suffer or permit any waste or strip thereof; that he will keep said premises free from mechanic's and all other liens and save the seller harmless therefrom and reimburse seller for all costs and attorney's fees incurred by him in defending against any such liens; that he will pay all taxes hereafter levied against said property, as well as all water rents, public charges and municipal liens which hereafter lawfully may be imposed upon said premises, all promptly before the same or any part thereof become past due; that at buyer's expense, he will insure and keep insured all buildings now or hereafter erected on said premises against loss or damage by fire (with extended coverage) in an amount not less than 80% of replacement cost in a company or companies satisfactory to the seller, with loss payable first to the seller and then to the buyer as their respective interests may appear and all policies of insurance to be delivered to the seller as soon as insured. Now if the buyer shall fail to pay any such liens, costs, water rents, taxes, or charges or to procure and pay for such insurance, the seller may do so and any payment so made shall be added to and become a part of the debt secured by this contract and shall bear interest at the rate aforesaid, without waiver, however, of any right arising to the seller for buyer's breach of contract.

The seller agrees that at his expense and within 21 days from the date hereof, he will furnish unto buyer a title insurance policy insuring (in an amount equal to said purchase price) marketable title in and to said premises in the seller on or subsequent to the date of this agreement, save and except the usual printed exceptions and the building and other restrictions and easements now of record, if any. Seller also agrees that when said purchase price is fully paid and upon request and upon surrender of this agreement, he will deliver a good and sufficient deed conveying said premises in fee simple unto the buyer, his heirs and assigns, free and clear of encumbrances as of the date hereof and free and clear of all encumbrances since said date placed, permitted or arising by, through or under seller, excepting, however, the said easements and restrictions and the taxes, municipal liens, water rents and public charges so assumed by the buyer and further excepting all liens and encumbrances created by the buyer or his assigns.

(Continued on reverse)

*IMPORTANT NOTICE: Delete, by lining out, whichever phrase and whichever warranty (A) or (B) is not applicable. If warranty (A) is applicable and if the seller is a creditor, as such word is defined in the Truth-in-Lending Act and Regulation Z, the seller MUST comply with the Act and Regulation by making required disclosures; for this purpose, use Stevens-Ness Form No. 1308 or similar unless the contract will become a first lien to finance the purchase of a dwelling in which event use Stevens-Ness Form No. 1307 or similar.

Sam Seller and Betty Seller
123 S. E. Quiet Street
Portland, Oregon 97238
SELLER'S NAME AND ADDRESS

Bruce Buyer and Sally Buyer
123 S. E. Quiet Street
Portland, Oregon 97238
BUYER'S NAME AND ADDRESS

After recording return to:

Bruce Buyer and Sally Buyer
123 S. E. Quiet Street
Portland, Oregon 97238
NAME, ADDRESS, ZIP

Until a change is requested all tax statements shall be sent to the following address.

123 S. E. Quiet Street
Portland, Oregon 97238
NAME, ADDRESS, ZIP

SPACE RESERVED
FOR
RECORDER'S USE

STATE OF OREGON,
}
ss.
County of
I certify that the within instrument was received for record on the day of , 19 , at o'clock M., and recorded in book on page or as file/reel number ,
Record of Deeds of said county.
Witness my hand and seal of County affixed.

Recording Officer
By Deputy

38

SAMPLE #8 — Continued

And it is understood and agreed between said parties that time is of the essence of this contract, and in case the buyer shall fail to make the payments above required, or any of them, punctually within 20 days of the time limited therefor, or fail to keep any agreement herein contained, then the seller at his option shall have the following rights: (1) to declare this contract null and void, (2) to declare the whole unpaid principal balance of said purchase price with the interest thereon at once due and payable, (3) to withdraw said deed and other documents from escrow and/or (4) to foreclose this contract by suit in equity, and in any of such cases, all rights and interest created or then existing in favor of the buyer as against the seller hereunder shall utterly cease and determine and the right to the possession of the premises above described and all other rights acquired by the buyer hereunder shall revert to and revest in said seller without any act of re-entry, or any other act of said seller to be performed and without any right of the buyer of return, reclamation or compensation for moneys paid on account of the purchase of said property as absolutely, fully and perfectly as if this contract and such payments had never been made; and in case of such default all payments theretofore made on this contract are to be retained by and belong to said seller as the agreed and reasonable rent of said premises up to the time of such default. And the said seller, in case of such default, shall have the right immediately, or at any time thereafter, to enter upon the land aforesaid, without any process of law, and take immediate possession thereof, together with all the improvements and appurtenances thereon or thereto belonging.

The buyer further agrees that failure by the seller at any time to require performance by the buyer of any provision hereof shall in no way affect his right hereunder to enforce the same, nor shall any waiver by said seller of any breach of any provision hereof be held to be a waiver of any succeeding breach of any such provision, or as a waiver of the provision itself.

The true and actual consideration paid for this transfer, stated in terms of dollars, is $ 55,000.00 ⓧⓧⓧⓧⓧⓧⓧⓧⓧⓧⓧⓧⓧⓧⓧⓧⓧⓧⓧⓧⓧⓧⓧⓧⓧⓧⓧⓧⓧⓧⓧⓧⓧⓧⓧⓧⓧⓧ

In case suit or action is instituted to foreclose this contract or to enforce any provision hereof, the losing party in said suit or action agrees to pay such sum as the trial court may adjudge reasonable as attorney's fees to be allowed the prevailing party in said suit or action and if an appeal is taken from any judgment or decree of such trial court, the losing party further promises to pay such sum as the appellate court shall adjudge reasonable as the prevailing party's attorney's fees on such appeal.

In construing this contract, it is understood that the seller or the buyer may be more than one person or a corporation; that if the context so requires, the singular pronoun shall be taken to mean and include the plural, the masculine, the feminine and the neuter, and that generally all grammatical changes shall be made, assumed and implied to make the provisions hereof apply equally to corporations and to individuals.

This agreement shall bind and inure to the benefit of, as the circumstances may require, not only the immediate parties hereto but their respective heirs, executors, administrators, personal representatives, successors in interest and assigns as well.

IN WITNESS WHEREOF, said parties have executed this instrument in triplicate; if either of the undersigned is a corporation, it has caused its corporate name to be signed and its corporate seal affixed hereto by its officers duly authorized thereunto by order of its board of directors.

Sam Seller _Sam Seller_ Bruce Buyer _Bruce Buyer_

Betty Seller _Betty Seller_ Sally Buyer _Sally Buyer_

NOTE—The sentence between the symbols ①, if not applicable, should be deleted. See ORS 93.030).

STATE OF OREGON,)
County of Multnomah } ss.
September 29 , 19 90 .
Personally appeared the above named
Sam Seller, Betty Seller, Bruce Buyer and Sally Buyer
and acknowledged the foregoing instrument to be their voluntary act and deed.
Before me:
(OFFICIAL SEAL) Thomas C. Sojac
Notary Public for Oregon
My commission expires Nov. 7, 1992

STATE OF OREGON, County of) ss.
...................., 19....... .
Personally appeared .... and
.... who, being duly sworn,
each for himself and not one for the other, did say that the former is the
.... president and that the latter is the
.... secretary of
.... a corporation,
and that the seal affixed to the foregoing instrument is the corporate seal
of said corporation and that said instrument was signed and sealed in behalf of said corporation by authority of its board of directors; and each of them acknowledged said instrument to be its voluntary act and deed.
Before me:
(SEAL)
Notary Public for Oregon
My commission expires:

ORS 93.635 (1) All instruments contracting to convey fee title to any real property, at a time more than 12 months from the date that the instrument is executed and the parties are bound, shall be acknowledged, in the manner provided for acknowledgment of deeds, by the conveyor of the title to be conveyed. Such instruments, or a memorandum thereof, shall be recorded by the conveyor not later than 15 days after the instrument is executed and the parties are bound thereby.
ORS 93.990(3) Violation of ORS 93.635 is punishable, upon conviction, by a fine of not more than $100.

ⓧⓧⓧⓧⓧⓧⓧⓧⓧⓧⓧⓧⓧⓧ)

Additional Terms

Seller is purchasing the premises by means of a mortgage recorded July 13, 1975 Book 1738, Page 94, Mortgage Records, of which the mortgagee is Oregon Mutual Savings Bank. Seller shall keep and pay the mortgage according to its terms. Should seller default, buyer may make the payments and receive credit as if made on this contract.

The premises are subject to:
1. Covenants, conditions and restrictions imposed by instrument recorded April 1, 1975 in Book 1714, Page 593, Deed Records.
2. Ten foot utility easement over the east 10 feet as shown on recorded plat.

Buyer is purchasing the premises in their present condition, "as is" based upon his own independent inspection and judgment and does not rely upon any representation of seller or seller's agent.

b. CONVENTIONAL FINANCING

By this method of financing, a lending institution agrees to lend the money without a government guarantee that it will pay off the remainder of the debt if there is a default.

Under conventional financing, the greater the down payment, the less the interest rate because the lending institution feels more secure with greater equity in the real property. But keep in mind what has been discussed in chapter 1 about buying a house at the maximum limit. The same also applies to making as small a down payment as possible. By making as small a down payment as possible, the buyer has extra funds to spend elsewhere. And when you, as buyer, decide to sell, it may be easier to find another buyer to take over your equity if it is fairly small. But if you have a large equity buildup because of a large down payment, it will generally be harder to find a buyer to take over your equity.

1. How much down payment?

Under conventional financing a larger down payment is normally required than under FHA or VA financing. How much this will be depends upon the mortgage and real estate market at any given time. It could be anywhere from 3% of the purchase price up to 20% or more. Normally, you can expect to be required to pay about 5% of the total price, plus closing costs. If you are approved by the lender for 5% financing, you should have this money available at the time of closing.

You should also keep in mind that generally you will pay a higher interest rate with a conventional loan than you would with an FHA or VA loan. At certain times, however, conventional financing may, in fact, be better than FHA or VA financed loans. You should shop around to find the best type of financing since market conditions do vary.

2. Loan placement fee

Under conventional financing the commercial lender charges a "loan placement fee" also called a "loan service fee" or a "loan charge." The reason given for this is because of the expense involved in processing the loan. The amount charged certainly makes that argument debatable. It has been characterized by some as a fee which the lender charges for the privilege and expense of using its money. This fee can be anywhere from 1% to 3% or more, depending upon the amount borrowed and the amount of the down payment. Two percent is average. But, here again, the less the loan fee is, the higher the interest is and vice versa. The loan fee is a one-time charge assessed against the buyer as one of the expenses for the buyer's closing costs. For example, on a $75,000 loan where the lending institution charges a loan service fee of 1%, the purchaser will pay a loan service fee of $750 ($75,000 x .01%) = $750.

c. FHA

The Federal Housing Administration (FHA) is a federal agency which insures the lender against any loss on the loan if the buyer becomes unable to pay. It insures the lender, not the borrower. To protect against nonpayment, it requires the lender to comply with certain terms and conditions. For instance, it requires the lender to lend at a certain rate of interest on the loan, which is usually less than the rate of interest in the conventional market.

You can find out the present FHA interest rate by calling your local Federal Housing Administration office. When you are ready to purchase your home under FHA, you should then contact a lender and indicate that you wish to have an FHA insured mortgage. This should be done at the time you find your house. And you should also specify in the earnest money agreement that the purchase is subject to approval of the FHA financing.

1. Mortgage insurance premium

The purchaser should be prepared to pay an average of 3.8% of the sale price (added on to the debt) or a 3.2% charge (paid at closing) for mortgage insurance. FHA requires this in addition to the purchase price in order to provide a reserve fund to protect the lender against loss if the purchaser defaults on the loan payment. If this charge is added to the debt, your monthly payment will increase.

2. Discount points

Because the FHA maximum interest is generally lower than the conventional interest, lenders attempt to make up the difference by charging "points." A "point" is $1 per $100 of the mortgage loan amount or 1%. It is a one-time interest charge which is deducted at the outset. The number of points which the lender charges will vary with the number of factors such as the availability of money and the cost of money to the lender. The points may range anywhere from 2 to 6. Under FHA regulations, the purchaser is allowed to pay the discount points and so is the seller. This can be a subject for negotiation when making the purchase contract. You must be cautious when selling under FHA or VA because you can be charged for unexpected expenses and costs. Before you agree to such a sale, consult with someone knowledgeable about these costs so you can negotiate about them with understanding. Insist that all costs be disclosed in advance of signing the earnest money agreement.

There are times, however, when a seller would find it advantageous to sell under FHA or VA financing. As a seller, you should examine the prevailing market conditions to determine whether selling FHA or VA would be in your best interests. Also, a knowledgeable real estate agent, broker, or lender in whom you have confidence could provide invaluable assistance. Keep in mind that they will expect to be compensated, but you could make it up in savings.

3. Mortgage limits for FHA financing

Under present FHA financing, the buyer can secure an FHA loan to purchase a home up to the following percentages of appraised value:

97% of the first $25,000

95% of the rest of the allowable amount of a loan. (This varies from region to region, as do prices. Portland currently has a maximum amount of $94,000).

At one time FHA loans were assumable without restriction. Now, however, these "blind assumptions" are prohibited during the first year and restricted thereafter. Consult your lender, read your loan papers, and consult professionals if uncertain.

d. VETERANS ADMINISTRATION LOANS (VA)

After World War II, the federal government set up the Veterans Administration to, among other things, assist veterans in financing the purchase of their homes. The program was so successful that it was continued. If you are a veteran, you may qualify under VA financing. If you seek VA financing, you first must apply for a Certificate of Eligibility by submitting your discharge papers. If qualified, you will receive a certificate from the Veterans Administration.

Under a VA loan, the Veterans Administration *guarantees* 75% of the loan. This is different from FHA, which only *insures* the loan. For the purposes of this text it is not critical to know the distinction, but in the event of a default (where you are unable to continue to make payments) under an FHA loan you become liable for the remaining loan balance, but FHA historically has not sought a deficiency judgment against the defaulting buyer. A definite change in this procedure is on the horizon, so don't count on this lasting too much longer.

In the Veterans Administration, on the other hand, it has been the usual practice to secure a personal judgment against a defaulting borrower where the sale of the house upon foreclosure was not sufficient to pay off the debt. There are instances where the Veterans Administration will "forgive" or "cancel" the loan. These are unusual circumstances, but the procedure is available.

When I wrote the first edition I stated:

> Although the defaulting homeowner may be subject to a personal judgment over conventional or FHA financing, as a practical matter, the mortgagee (lender) usually takes the house back in satisfaction of the debt owed and does not attempt to secure a deficiency judgment against the mortgagor (buyer) since there is usually enough equity

43

in the house to resell it so that the lender does not lose any money.

That was in 1980. Since then, tens of thousands of foreclosures and defaults without foreclosure took place in Oregon. Equities vanished as prices dropped. Lenders suffered severe losses. It is safe to say today that a lender will not voluntarily take back the defaulted property in satisfaction of the debt. In fact, the lender may not take it back at all. Instead, the lender will foreclose and, if available, seek to collect any deficiency against the borrower.

e. SECOND MORTGAGES/SECOND TRUST DEEDS (FROM THE SELLER'S STANDPOINT)

Suppose the buyer of your property does not have enough money to make the down payment. Should you take a second mortgage? Sometimes the salesperson or buyer will suggest this. The idea is that the amount of cash down together with the amount of the second mortgage will equal the down payment required by the lender.

Before you agree to this, take into account two things:

(a) The professional lender through years of experience knows what standards and requirements to set to establish the creditworthiness of the loan. They know what is a safe credit risk. Can you afford to take a chance that a bank would not take?

(b) A second mortgage (or deed of trust) is no good if the buyer fails to keep up the payments on the first. Then, the holder of the first mortgage will foreclose not only on the defaulting buyer but also on you, the holder of the second. You could well end up with nothing.

There is another way a second mortgage can come up. You own real estate having a market value of $85,000 with a $60,000 debt against it — thus an equity of $25,000. Bob Buyer, who is willing to pay $85,000, suggests you deed the property to him and that he assume your loan. But, Mr. Buyer has only $15,000 cash, $10,000 less than is necessary to cash you out. He suggests that you take a "second" for that $10,000. This proposal has all of the risks mentioned above, and it is foolish because there is a better way — a device called a "wraparound."

What you do is sell on a contract for the full price of $85,000 but agree to pay and maintain the mortgage debt. Your contract is said to wrap around the mortgage debt, hence the name. As far as you and the buyer (but not the first lender) are concerned, you are in first place. Should the buyer default, you can foreclose and take the property back (of course with the mortgage still on it). Wraparounds can be neat devices especially if the interest rate you charge on the contract is higher than the interest you pay on the mortgage.

f. INTEREST

1. How much?

Generally, most installment sales bear interest on the unpaid portion of the purchase price.

Oregon no longer has any limitation on the amount of interest a lender or seller can charge. In other words, usury no longer exists.

Professional lenders must comply with the federal "Truth in Lending Law," which requires certain disclosures and a statement of the annual percentage rate (APR). This rate usually is higher than that stated in the note because it includes items not considered as interest outside of that law, such as loan costs. The object of this law is to give people an opportunity to "shop" for money as they would shop for anything else.

In practice, it does not work that way, because by the time a buyer finds out the true interest rate, so much time has elapsed, that the purchase will be lost if he or she tries to find another loan. What happens is this. The buyer does not receive the truth-in-lending disclosure until ten days before the sale is to be closed. (Ten days is the minimum time required by law.) By that time the buyer has paid a loan application fee, waited for several weeks while the application was being processed and is rapidly approaching the deadline for concluding the sale. Most buyers are not inclined to make a second loan application under these circumstances.

Fortunately many lenders, if requested, will *prior to application* give to a prospective borrower the estimated loan costs. Remember, these costs include these components:

(a) The cost of obtaining the loan
(b) The interest rate
(c) The costs of getting out of the loan (pre-payment penalties and assumption fees)

This estimate, while it is not strict compliance with the truth-in-lending law, will enable a borrower to know in advance what the loan costs will be. A good real estate salesperson or broker will assist a buyer-borrower to obtain and to interpret this information.

2. Variable interest rates

With a variable rate mortgage, a basic interest rate is agreed upon but after that the rate will vary according to an index of money costs published by the Federal Home Loan Bank Board. Interest rates can be adjusted up or down at specified intervals. Usually there is a stated maximum that the rate can increase and no limit on decreases. These loans are often called "adjusted rate mortgages," or ARMs. There are many variations among ARMs and because of their intricate nature it is difficult to compare one with the other or with fixed rate mortgages to determine which is your best value. If you are considering a variable rate mortgage, it is best to consult with a qualified person.

We have had approximately ten years of experience with variable rate mortgages, enough to give some idea of their pitfalls. Be warned of this: the initial ARM interest rate alone is not a good indicator of the interest you will pay. The initial interest rate is often artificially low as an inducement — a loss leader — to get you to take out the loan. Therefore, don't be misled by the initial rate. Instead, ask what the rate would be, based on the present index, on the second anniversary of the loan.

If you decide you still want an ARM, look at the starting interest rate, the index to be used, the margin (that is the difference between the rate charged and the index to which it is tied), the maximum annual increase, and the maximum total increase. In addition, look at all of the origination fees and costs, not just the loan fee. Lenders have become very adept at finding new categories of costs to charge borrowers up front.

g. CLOSING COSTS

Most buyers will apply to a bank, savings and loan association or mortgage company for their loans. These lenders will usually charge them closing costs which can add up substantially. Closing costs include charges for:

(a) Title insurance

(b) Survey

(c) Preparation of documents

(d) Credit report

(e) Closing fee

(f) Service or loan fee, usually a percentage of the loan

(g) Mortgage discount (however, in FHA or VA transactions the buyer is not allowed to pay this amount)

(h) Appraisal fee

(i) Recording fee

(j) Mortgage insurance premium

(k) Escrow fees

(l) Fire insurance premiums

(m) Adjustments for prepaid items such as prepaid taxes and insurance

(n) Miscellaneous charges for photographs, inspections, payment schedules, and the like

(o) Tax and fire insurance premium deposits which are added to with each monthly payment. Oregon requires a lender, in some circumstances, to pay the borrower's interest on these funds. If you are not receiving interest, make inquiries. (However, Oregon law does not affect federally sponsored financing.)

(p) Document preparation fee

(q) Government service fee

6

CLOSING THE DEAL

a. TITLE INSURANCE

In most sales of real estate the seller agrees at his or her expense to furnish the buyer with a title insurance policy (usually called "title policies") insuring the seller's title for the amount of the purchase price. There is a misconception that this is required by law. It is really a matter of tradition and negotiation.

Never buy without getting title insurance! But never be lulled into a false sense of security because you are getting it. While title insurance companies (called "title companies") do operate honestly, they also take care of their own interests first. Therefore, ask for and obtain the preliminary title report (often simply called "title") as soon as possible. Most buyers do not even see it until closing, if at all.

The title insurance company will examine the title clear back to the time it was first owned and will issue a preliminary title report which describes the condition of the seller's title (see Sample #9). Notice its basic structure:

(a) The name of the owner, called the vestee

(b) The legal description of the property

(c) The amount of the latest yearly taxes and whether they are paid

(d) Any circumstances which are in exception to the vestee having a free and clear title (called "exceptions")

(e) A map outlining the property boundaries

All of it should be studied, particularly the exceptions. The exceptions include such things as easements, deed restrictions, mortgages, liens, covenants, and the like. These things are not necessarily bad, and, in fact, may well be beneficial to the property. Most urban real estate will have one or more of these kind of exceptions. What's important is that you are not getting an exception you do not want or expect. You may find, for instance, that one of the exceptions is a lien of judgment against the seller. If you were to buy without removal of the lien, you would own the property subject to the lien instead of free and clear. Simply because you find an unwanted exception is no reason to be upset; just be careful. Most of the time these can be eliminated — often from the proceeds of the sale if you specify that the title you get will be free of them.

If the title report contains exceptions such as easements or deed restrictions and conditions, ask the title company for a copy of them if their contents are not set out in the report. Read them carefully to be sure you are getting all you expect. You may or may not want sewer line or power line easements through your property!

Title insurance policies also contain printed exceptions. These do not appear on the title report. Like most insurance policies, they contain standard wording that is very technical. These standard exceptions are printed in Sample #10. Read them. You will discover that many things are not insured. Among them are land use laws and ordinances, easements not shown on public records, conflicts in boundary lines, facts which can be ascertained by inspection of the land or inquiring of persons in possession, and so on.

By regulation, a title insurance policy, when issued, must be for the full amount of the sale price. Modern policies also contain an inflation protection endorsement which automatically increases upward the amount of insurance by a percentage equal to the increased cost of construction according to the Construction Cost Index published by the United States Department of Commerce.

Title companies also take some hidden risks. How do you know that the nice person selling that house really owns it? Is it just a renter fraudulently claiming to be the owner? You don't know. Your protection is title insurance which

SAMPLE #9
PRELIMINARY TITLE REPORT

SAFECO TITLE INSURANCE COMPANY

Office __1800 S.W. First Ave.__   REPORT NO. __22222__
__Portland, Ore.   97201__
225-1005

PRELIMINARY REPORT FOR:

John Gilbert	Standard Owners	$ 27,500.00 Prem. $ 154.00
Attorney at Law	Standard Purchasers $	Prem. $
Portland, Oregon	Standard Lenders $ 22,000.00 Prem. $ 25.00
	ALTA Lenders $	Prem. $

We are prepared to issue a title insurance policy in the form and amount shown above insuring the title to the following described land:

Lot 5, Block 4, HAZELWOOD TERRACES, in the City of Portland, Multnomah County, Oregon.

Vestee: JOHN SULLIVAN and MARY SULLIVAN, as tenants by the entirety

Dated as of   September 1   1990   at 8:00 a.m.

SAFECO TITLE INSURANCE COMPANY

By _____
   J. Klinefelter
                              Title Officer

Subject to the printed exceptions, exclusions and stipulations which are part of said policy, and to the following:

1. Taxes for the fiscal year 1989-90   delinquent.
    Original Amount: $542.54, plus interest.
    Account No.:   3456-2210

2. City lien in favor of the City of Portland.
    For: Street improvement
    Dated: June 14, 1986
    Entered in Bond Docket: 54, Page 335
    Original Amount: $1,452.00
    Payable in 20 semi-annual installments with 2 semi-annual installments
    paid, balance, plus interest, unpaid.

SAMPLE #9 — Continued

3. An easement created by instrument, including the terms and provisions thereof.
   Dated: June 21, 1963.
   Recorded: July 5, 1963, in Book 542, Page 31, Deed Records.
   In Favor Of: PORTLAND POWER AND LIGHT COMPANY.
   For: Utility purposes.
   Affects: The West five (5) feet.

4. Covenants, Conditions, Restrictions and Easements, but omitting restrictions, if any, based on race, color, religion or national origin, imposed by instrument, including the terms and provisions thereof, recorded August 5, 1963, in Book 565, Page 42, Deed Records.

5. Mortgage, including the terms and provisions thereof, given to secure an indebtedness with interest thereon and such future advances as may be provided therein.
   Dated: July 3, 1963.
   Recorded: August 6, 1963, in Book 400, Page 332, Mortgage Records.
   Amount: $12,000.00.
   Mortgagor: QUALITY BUILDERS, Inc., an Oregon corporation.
   Mortgagee: FIRST FEDERAL SAVINGS & LOAN ASSOCIATION.

6. Real Estate Contract, including the terms and provisions thereof dated September 14, 1965, recorded October 1, 1965, in Book 744, Page 341, Deed Records, between HARVEY COLLINS, Vendor and MABEL H. WILKINS, Vendee.

   The Vendors interest in said Real Estate Contract was assigned by instrument, dated November 2, 1966, recorded November 3, 1966, in Book 813, Page 541, Deed Records to JOHN SULLIVAN and MARY SULLIVAN, husband and wife.

7. Due probate and administration of the Estate of MABEL H. WILKINS, deceased, Probate No. 103561, which proceedings are pending in the Circuit Court for Multnomah County. GLADYS WILKINS was appointed as personal representative and has power to execute the forthcoming conveyance. Attorney for estate, JOHN GILBERT.

8. Pending dissolution of marriage proceedings in the Circuit Court for Multnomah County, Suit No. 751097, entitled JOHN SULLIVAN, Petitioner, vs. MARY SULLIVAN, Respondant, and attorney's lien of JIM HOLSTROM arising therefrom.

SAMPLE #9 — Continued

NOTE A: We find the following unsatisfied judgement docketed against name similar to ALBERT JONES.

A Judgement for the amount herein stated and any other amounts due.
Register No.: 51302
Entered: May 4, 1977
Docket Book: 51, Page 13, Line 2
Amount: $100.00 per month child support
(Payment current through September 1, 1984).
Debtor: ALBERT J. JONES
Creditor: ALICE WETZEL
Attorney for Creditor: RALPH BROWN

NOTE B: We find no judgements or United States Internal Revenue liens against RUTH JONES.

PRELIMINARY REPORT ONLY

insures you if the deed is forged or if the seller is later found to be mentally ill and legally unable to sign a deed.

The necessity is obvious. Even the owners of casinos in Las Vegas insist on getting title insurance; they know the odds.

One warning: it is not unusual for a seller to tell a buyer, "You don't need title insurance, I have it." Don't be fooled. The seller's policy is not only outdated, but it insures the seller's interest, not yours.

b. MORTGAGE INSURANCE

If you are borrowing money from a mortgage company to buy the property, you will be required to provide the lender with a title insurance policy insuring its mortgage just as your title is insured. This is generally done by an endorsement on the title policy that the seller gives the buyer, and it costs $25 regardless of the amount of the mortgage. In many cases, the borrower must provide an A.L.T.A. (American Lend Title Association) policy, which gives lenders a broader coverage than ordinary title insurance. It also costs more. A mortgage title insurance policy does not protect the owner or buyer, only the lender. Don't rely on it only.

c. ESCROW

It is fair to say that the vast number of transactions close in escrow. There is nothing mysterious about the term. It's just that it has no synonym. Literally, it means a piece of parchment (scroll). In the modern sense, it means to deposit a deed with one person for delivery to another upon fulfillment of a condition.

1. Choosing an escrow agent

Escrow agents, with certain exceptions, such as banks and lawyers, must be licensed to operate as such through the Oregon Real Estate Department. These businesses are regulated, bonded, and audited, and have generally done a

SAMPLE #10
TITLE INSURANCE POLICY

POLICY OF TITLE INSURANCE POLICY

issued by

SAFECO TITLE INSURANCE COMPANY

a California corporation, hereinafter called the Company, for a valuable consideration paid for this policy of title insurance, the number, date, and amount of which are shown in Schedule A, does hereby insure the parties named as Insured in Schedule A, the heirs, devisees, personal representatives of such Insured, or if a corporation, its successors by dissolution, merger or consolidation, against direct loss or damage not exceeding the amount stated in Schedule A, together with costs, attorneys' fees and expenses which the Company may be obligated to pay as provided in the Conditions and Stipulations hereof, which the Insured shall sustain by reason of:

1. Title to the land described in Schedule A being vested, at the date hereof, otherwise than as herein stated; or

2. Unmarketability, at the date hereof, of the title to said land of any vestee named herein, unless such unmarketability exists because of defects, liens, encumbrances, or other matters shown or referred to in Schedule B; or

3. Any defect in, or lien or encumbrance on, said title existing at the date hereof, not shown or referred to in Schedule B, or excluded from coverage in the Schedule of Exclusions from Coverage; or

4. Any defect in the execution of any mortgage or deed of trust shown in Schedule B securing an indebtedness, the owner of which is insured by this policy, but only insofar as such defect affects the lien or charge of such mortgage or deed of trust upon said land; or

5. Priority, at the date hereof, over any such mortgage or deed of trust, of any lien or encumbrance upon said land, except as shown in Schedule B such mortgage or deed of trust being shown in the order of its priority,

all subject, however, to the Schedule of Exclusions from Coverage and the Conditions and Stipulations hereto annexed which, together with Schedules A and B, are hereby made a part of this policy.

In Witness Whereof, SAFECO Title Insurance Company has caused its corporate name and seal to be hereunto affixed by its duly authorized officers as of Date of Policy shown in Schedule A.

Bruce M. Jones
Secretary

W H Little
President

An Authorized Signature

SAMPLE #10 — Continued

SCHEDULE OF EXCLUSIONS FROM COVERAGE

This policy does not insure against loss or damage by reason of the following:

1. Any law, ordinance or governmental regulation (including but not limited to building and zoning ordinances) restricting or regulating or prohibiting the occupancy, use or enjoyment of the land, or regulating the character, dimensions, or location of any improvement now or hereafter erected on said land, or prohibiting a separation in ownership or a reduction in the dimensions or area of any lot or parcel of land.
2. Governmental rights of police power or eminent domain unless notice of the exercise of such rights appears in the public records at the date hereof.
3. Title to any property beyond the lines of the land expressly described in Schedule A or title to streets, roads, avenues, lanes, ways or waterways on which such land abuts, or the right to maintain therein vaults, tunnels, ramps or any other structure or improvement; or any rights or easements therein unless this policy specifically provides that such property, rights or easements are insured, except that if the land abuts upon one or more physically open streets or highways this policy insures the ordinary rights of abutting owners for access to one of such streets or highways, unless otherwise excepted or excluded herein.
4. Defects, liens, encumbrances, adverse claims against the title as insured or other matters (1) created, suffered, assumed or agreed to by the Insured claiming loss or damage; or (2) known to the Insured Claimant either at the date of this policy or at the date such Insured Claimant acquired an estate or interest insured by this policy and not shown by the public records, unless disclosure thereof in writing by the Insured shall have been made to the Company prior to the date of this policy; or (3) resulting in no loss to the Insured Claimant; or (4) attaching or created subsequent to the date hereof.
5. Loss or damage which would not have been sustained if the Insured were a purchaser or encumbrancer for value without knowledge.
6. Usury or claims of usury.
7. "Consumer credit protection," "truth-in-lending," or similar law.

CONDITIONS AND STIPULATIONS

1. Definition of Terms

The following terms when used in this policy mean:

(a) "land": the land described, specifically or by reference, in Schedule A and improvements affixed thereto which by law constitute real property;

(b) "public records": those records which impart constructive notice of matters relating to said land;

(c) "knowledge": actual knowledge, not constructive knowledge or notice which may be imputed to the Insured by reason of any public records;

(d) "date": the effective date;

(e) "mortgage": mortgage, deed of trust, trust deed, or other security instrument: and

(f) "insured": the party or parties named as Insured, and if the owner of the indebtedness secured by a mortgage shown in Schedule B is named as an Insured in Schedule A, the Insured shall include (1) each successor in interest in ownership of such indebtedness, (2) any such owner who acquires the estate or interest referred to in this policy by foreclosure, trustee's sale, or other legal manner in satisfaction of said indebtedness, and (3) any federal agency or instrumentality which is an insurer or guarantor under an insurance contract or guaranty insuring or guaranteeing said indebtedness, or any part thereof, whether named as an Insured herein or not, subject otherwise to the provisions hereof.

2. Benefits after Acquisition of Title

If an insured owner of the indebtedness secured by a mortgage described in Schedule B acquires said estate or interest, or any part thereof, by foreclosure, trustee's sale, or other legal manner in satisfaction of said indebtedness, or any part thereof, or if a federal agency or instrumentality acquires said estate or interest, or any part thereof, as a consequence of an insurance contract or guaranty insuring or guaranteeing the indebtedness secured by this policy, or any part thereof, this policy shall continue in force

in favor of such Insured, agency or instrumentality, subject to all of the conditions and stipulations hereof.

3. Defense and Prosecution of Actions — Notice of Claim to be Given by the Insured

(a) The Company, at its own cost and without undue delay shall provide (1) for the defense of the Insured in all litigation consisting of actions or proceedings commenced against the Insured, or defenses, restraining orders, or injunctions interposed against a foreclosure or sale of the mortgage and indebtedness covered by this policy or a sale of the estate or interest in said land; or (2) for such action as may be appropriate to establish the title of the estate or interest or the lien of the mortgage as insured, which litigation or action in any of such events is founded upon an alleged defect, lien or encumbrance insured against by this policy, and may pursue any litigation to final determination in the court of last resort.

(b) In case any such action or proceeding shall be begun, or defense interposed, or in case knowledge shall come to the Insured of any claim of title or interest which is adverse to the title of the estate or interest or lien of the mortgage as insured, or which might cause loss or damage for which the Company shall or may be liable by virtue of this policy, or if the Insured shall in good faith contract to sell the indebtedness secured by a mortgage covered by this policy or, if an Insured in good faith leases or contracts to sell, lease or mortgage the same, or if the successful bidder at a foreclosure sale under a mortgage covered by this policy refuses to purchase and in any such event the title to said estate or interest is rejected as unmarketable, the Insured shall notify the Company thereof in writing. If such notice shall not be given to the Company within ten days of the receipt of process or pleadings or if the Insured shall not, in writing, promptly notify the Company of any defect, lien or encumbrance insured against which shall come to the knowledge of the Insured, or if the Insured shall not, in writing, promptly notify the Company of any such rejection by reason of claimed unmarketability of title, then all liability of the Company in regard to the subject

matter of such action, proceeding or matter shall cease and terminate; provided, however, that failure to notify shall in no case prejudice the claim of any Insured unless the Company shall be actually prejudiced by such failure and then only to the extent of such prejudice.

(c) The Company shall have the right at its own cost to institute and prosecute any action or proceeding or do any other act which in its opinion may be necessary or desirable to establish the title of the estate or interest or the lien of the mortgage as insured; and the Company may take any appropriate action under the terms of this policy whether or not it shall be liable thereunder and shall not thereby concede liability or waive any provision of this policy.

(d) In all cases where this policy permits or requires the Company to prosecute or provide for the defense of any action or proceeding, the Insured shall secure to it the right to so prosecute or provide defense in such action or proceeding, and all appeals therein, and permit it to use, at its option, the name of the Insured for such purpose. Whenever requested by the Company the Insured shall give the Company all reasonable aid in any such action or proceeding, in effecting settlement, securing evidence, obtaining witnesses, or prosecuting or defending such action or proceeding, and the Company shall reimburse the Insured for any expense so incurred.

4. Notice of Loss — Limitation of Action

In addition to the notices required under paragraph 4(b), a statement in writing of any loss or damage for which it is claimed the Company is liable under this policy shall be furnished to the Company within sixty days after such loss or damage shall have been determined and no right of action shall accrue to the Insured under this policy until thirty days after such statement shall have been furnished, and no recovery shall be had by the Insured under this policy unless action shall be commenced thereon within five years after expiration of said thirty day period. Failure to furnish such statement of loss or damage, or to commence such action within the time hereinbefore specified, shall

(Conditions and Stipulations Continued and Concluded on Last Page of This Policy)

P-218-A-Oregon (G.S.) Rev. 7-74
Standard Coverage Policy Form

SCHEDULE A

Date of
Policy: **September 14,** 1990

Amount $ 55,000.00

Policy No. **22222**
Premium $ 151.00

1. Name of Insured

   ALBERT JONES and RUTH JONES.

2. The estate or interest in the land described in this Schedule and which is covered by this policy is:

   A fee. *

3. The estate or interest referred to herein is at Date of Policy vested in

   ALBERT JONES and RUTH JONES,
   as tenants by the entirety.   **

4. The land referred to in this policy is described as

   Lot 5, Block 4, HAZELWOOD TERRACES, in the City
   of Portland, Multnomah County, Oregon.

---

*A "fee simple title" gives full right and title to the property. This is discussed in detail on page 71.
**Husband and wife together have an interest in the whole property.

SAMPLE #10 — Continued

P-218-B-Oregon (G.S.) Rev. 7-74
Standard Coverage Policy Form

SCHEDULE B

This policy does not insure against loss or damage, nor against costs, attorneys' fees or expenses, any or all of which arise by reason of the matters shown or referred to in this Schedule except to the extent that the owner of any mortgage or deed of trust is expressly insured on page 1 of this policy.

1. Taxes or assessments which are not shown as existing liens by the records of any taxing authority that levies taxes or assessments on real property or by public records; proceedings by a public agency which may result in taxes or assessments, or notices of such proceedings, whether or not shown by the records of such agency or by the public records.

2. Any facts, rights, interests, or claims which are not shown by the public records but which could be ascertained by an inspection of said land or by making inquiry of persons in possession thereof.

3. Easements, liens or encumbrances, or claims thereof, which are not shown by the public records; unpatented mining claims; reservations or exceptions in patents or in Acts authorizing the issuance thereof; water rights, claims or title to water.

4. Discrepancies, conflicts in boundary lines, shortage in area, encroachments or any other facts which a correct survey would disclose.

5. An easement created by instrument, including the terms and provisions thereof.
Dated: June 21, 1963.
Recorded: July 5, 1963, in Book 542, Page 31, Deed Records.
In favor of: PORTLAND POWER AND LIGHT COMPANY.
For: Utility purposes.
Affects: The West five feet (5').

6. Covenants, conditions, restrictions, and easements, but omitting restrictions, if any, based on race, color, religion or national origin, imposed by instrument, including the terms and provisions thereof, recorded August 5, 1963, in Book 565, Page 42, Deed Records.

7. Trust Deed, including the terms and provisions thereof, given to secure an indebtedness with interest thereon and such future advances as may be provided therein.
Dated: September 2, 1990
Recorded: September 14, 1990 in Book 931, Page 520, Mortgage Records.
Amount: $55,000.00.
Grantor: ALBERT JONES and RUTH JONES, husband and wife.
Trustee: SAFECO TITLE INSURANCE COMPANY.
Beneficiary: COMMERCE MORTGAGE COMPANY.

SAMPLE #10 — Continued

be a conclusive bar against maintenance by the Insured of any action under this policy.

5. Option to Pay, Settle or Compromise Claims

The Company shall have the option to pay or settle or compromise for or in the name of the Insured any claim insured against or to pay the full amount of this policy, or, in case loss is claimed under this policy by the owner of the indebtedness secured by a mortgage covered by this policy, the Company shall have the option to purchase said indebtedness; such purchase, payment or tender of payment of the full amount of this policy, together with all costs, attorneys' fees and expenses which the Company is obligated hereunder to pay, shall terminate all liability of the Company hereunder. In the event, after notice of claim has been given to the Company by the Insured, the Company offers to purchase said indebtedness, the owner of such indebtedness shall transfer and assign said indebtedness and the mortgage securing the same to the Company upon payment of the purchase price.

6. Payment of Loss

(a) The liability of the Company under this policy shall in no case exceed, in all, the actual loss of the Insured and costs and attorneys' fees which the Company may be obligated hereunder to pay.

(b) The Company will pay, in addition to any loss insured against by this policy, all cost imposed upon the Insured in litigation carried on by the Company for the Insured, and all costs and attorneys' fees in litigation carried on by the Insured with the written authorization of the Company.

(c) No claim for damages shall arise or be maintainable under this policy (1) if the Company, after having received notice of an alleged defect, lien or encumbrance not excepted or excluded herein removes such defect, lien or encumbrance within a reasonable time after receipt of such notice, or (2) for liability voluntarily assumed by the Insured in settling any claim or suit without written consent of the Company, or (3) in the event the title is rejected as unmarketable because of a defect, lien or encumbrance not excepted or excluded in this policy, until there has been a final determination by a court of competent jurisdiction sustaining such rejection.

(d) All payments under this policy, except payments made for costs, attorneys' fees and expenses, shall reduce the amount of the insurance pro tanto and no payment shall be made without producing this policy for endorsement of such payment unless the policy be lost or destroyed, in which case proof of such loss or destruction shall be furnished to the satisfaction of the Company; provided, however, if the owner of an indebtedness secured by a mortgage shown in Schedule B is an Insured herein then such payments shall not reduce pro tanto the amount of the insurance afforded hereunder as to such Insured, except to the extent that such payments reduce the amount of the indebtedness secured by such mortgage. Payment in full

by any person or voluntary satisfaction or release by the Insured of a mortgage covered by this policy shall terminate all liability of the Company to the insured owner of the indebtedness secured by such mortgage, except as provided in paragraph 2 hereof.

(e) When liability has been definitely fixed in accordance with the conditions of this policy the loss or damage shall be payable within thirty days thereafter.

7. Liability Noncumulative

It is expressly understood that the amount of this policy is reduced by any amount the Company may pay under any policy insuring the validity or priority of any mortgage shown or referred to in Schedule B hereof or any mortgage hereafter executed by the Insured which is a charge or lien on the estate or interest described or referred to in Schedule A, and the amount so paid shall be deemed a payment to the Insured under this policy. The provisions of this paragraph numbered 8 shall not apply to an Insured owner of an indebtedness secured by a mortgage shown in Schedule B unless such Insured acquires title to said estate or interest in satisfaction of said indebtedness or any part thereof.

8. Coinsurance and Apportionment

(a) In the event that a partial loss occurs after the Insured makes an improvement subsequent to the date of this policy, and only in that event, the Insured becomes a coinsurer to the extent hereinafter set forth.

If the cost of the improvement exceeds twenty per centum of the amount of this policy, such proportion only of any partial loss established shall be borne by the Company as one hundred twenty per centum of the amount of this policy bears to the sum of the amount of this policy and the amount expended for the improvement. The foregoing provisions shall not apply to costs and attorneys' fees incurred by the Company in prosecuting or providing for the defense of actions or proceedings in behalf of the Insured pursuant to the terms of this policy or to costs imposed on the Insured in such actions or proceedings, and shall apply only to that portion of losses which exceed in the aggregate ten per cent of the face of the policy.

Provided, however, that the foregoing coinsurance provisions shall not apply to any loss arising out of a lien or encumbrance for a liquidated amount which existed on the date of this policy and was not shown in Schedule B; and provided further, such coinsurance provisions shall not apply to any loss if, at the time of the occurrence of such loss, the then value of the premises, as so improved, does not exceed one hundred twenty per centum of the amount of this policy.

(b) If the land described or referred to in Schedule A is divisible into separate and noncontiguous parcels, or if contiguous and such parcels are not used as one single site, and a loss is established affecting one or more of said parcels but not all, the loss shall be computed and settled on a pro rata basis as if the face amount

of the policy was divided pro rata as to the value on the date of this policy of each separate independent parcel to the whole, exclusive of any improvements made subsequent to the date of this policy, unless a liability or value has otherwise been agreed upon as to each such parcel by the Company and the Insured at the time of the issuance of this policy and shown by an express statement herein or by an endorsement attached hereto.

9. Subrogation Upon Payment or Settlement

Whenever the Company shall have settled a claim under this policy, all right of subrogation shall vest in the Company unaffected by any act of the Insured, and it shall be subrogated to and be entitled to all rights and remedies which the Insured would have had against any person or property in respect to such claim had this policy not been issued. If the payment does not cover the loss of the Insured, the Company shall be subrogated to such rights and remedies in the proportion which said payment bears to the amount of said loss. If loss should result from any act of the Insured, such act shall not void this policy, but the Company, in that event, shall be required to pay only that part of any losses insured against hereunder which shall exceed the amount, if any, lost to the Company by reason of the impairment of the right of subrogation. The Insured, if requested by the Company, shall transfer to the Company all rights and remedies against any person or property necessary in order to perfect such right of subrogation, and shall permit the Company to use the name of the Insured in any transaction or litigation involving such rights or remedies.

If the Insured is the owner of the indebtedness secured by a mortgage covered by this policy, such Insured may release or substitute the personal liability of any debtor or guarantor, or extend or otherwise modify the terms of payment, or release a portion of the estate or interest from the lien of the mortgage, or release any collateral security for the indebtedness, provided such act does not result in any loss of priority of the lien of the mortgage.

10 Policy Entire Contract

Any action or actions or rights of action that the Insured may have or may bring against the Company arising out of the status of the lien of the mortgage covered by this policy or the title of the estate or interest insured herein must be based on the provisions of this policy.

No provision or condition of this policy can be waived or changed except by writing endorsed hereon or attached hereto signed by the President, a Vice President, the Secretary, an Assistant Secretary or other validating Officer of the Company.

11. Notices, Where Sent

All notices required to be given the Company and any statement in writing required to be furnished the Company shall be addressed to it at the office which issued this policy or to its Home Office, 13640 Roscoe Boulevard, Panorama City, California 91409.

P-218-Oregon (G.S.)

58

SAMPLE #10 — Continued

OWNER'S INFLATION PROTECTIVE INDORSEMENT NO. 3

Attached to Policy No.

Issued by

SAFECO TITLE INSURANCE COMPANY

The Company, recognizing the current effect of inflation on real property valuation and intending to provide additional monetary protection to the Insured Owner named in said Policy, hereby modifies said Policy, as follows:

1. Notwithstanding anything contained in said Policy to the contrary, the amount of insurance provided by said Policy, as stated in Schedule A thereof, is subject to cumulative annual upward adjustments in the manner and to the extent hereinafter specified.

2. "Adjustment Date" is defined, for the purpose of this Indorsement, to be 12:01 a.m. on the first January 1 which occurs more than six months after the Date of Policy, as shown in Schedule A of the Policy to which this Indorsement is attached and on each succeeding January 1.

3. An upward adjustment will be made on each of the Adjustment Dates, as defined above, by increasing the maximum of insurance provided by said Policy (as said amount may have been increased theretofore under the terms of this Indorsement) by the same percentage, if any, by which the United States Department of Commerce Composite Construction Cost Index (base period 1967) for the month of September immediately preceding exceeds such Index based upon the preceding year or any previous year; provided, however, that the maximum amount of insurance in force shall never exceed 175% of the amount of insurance stated in Schedule A of said Policy, less the amount of any claim paid under said Policy which, under the terms of the Conditions and Stipulations, reduces the amount of insurance in force. There shall be no annual adjustment in the amount of insurance for years in which there is no increase in said Construction Cost Index.

4. In the settlement of any claim against the Company under said Policy, the amount of insurance in force shall be deemed to be the amount which is in force as of the date on which the insured claimant first learned of the assertion or possible assertion of such claim, or as of the date of receipt by the Company of the first notice of such claim, whichever shall first occur.

Nothing herein contained shall be construed as extending or changing the effective date of said Policy.

This indorsement is made a part of said Policy and is subject to the schedules, conditions and stipulations therein, except as modified by the provisions hereof.

Dated:

SAFECO TITLE INSURANCE COMPANY

By...

Authorized Signature

P-283-Oregon 12-74
Owner's Inflation Protective Indorsement No. 3

competent and thorough job. The seller and buyer have the right to choose their own escrow agent — if you have a preference make it known to the realtor. Usually the realtor will guide you to his or her favorite. This is all right because you will get the best service there. But you are not bound to use the one the realtor recommends. However, whichever title company escrow service you use, it should be the same one that is going to issue the title insurance.

2. What an escrow agent does for you

In real estate, here's what happens. First, the seller deposits the deed or contract with the escrow agent with instructions to deliver it to the buyer when the buyer pays the purchase price. Then the buyer deposits the purchase price with the escrow agent with instructions to pay it to the seller when the seller delivers the deed and a good marketable title. When both conditions are met, the escrow agent pays the money to the seller and delivers the deed to the buyer. In effect, the escrow agent acts as a trustworthy go-between for the two parties.

This illustration, while essentially true, is actually an oversimplification. A lot more goes on.

The escrow agent receives the earnest money agreement from the broker, usually with an explanatory letter that first orders a preliminary title report. After receiving the title report and being certain the seller's title is in order with nothing unexpected against it, the escrow agent, based on the contents of the earnest money agreement, will prepare instructions for both seller and buyer to sign, and will prepare the necessary closing statements showing where the funds went and how the items were disbursed. The closing statements should be the mathematical equivalent of the instructions. Samples #11 to #14 illustrate the work of the escrow agent.

In preparing them, the escrow agent will make these adjustments to the price.

(a) Pro-rating of property taxes will result in an increase or decrease of the total cost. In Oregon, taxes are charged on the basis of the July 1 to June 30 fiscal year; they are payable with discount on November 15 (they are not overdue until May 15 of the next fiscal year). Unless a sale closes on July 1, some adjustment or pro-rate must be made. Essentially, all this means is that a person pays the taxes for the time he or she owns the property. If the seller, for instance, paid the taxes in full on November 15 and sells on the next January 15, the buyer will reimburse the prepaid taxes from that January 15 to the next June 30. Conversely, if a house is sold on September 15, before the taxes are paid, the seller will reimburse the buyer from past July 1 to that September 15. This is because the buyer will pay that period's taxes on November 15 along with taxes for the rest of the year.

(b) The cost of the title insurance premium will be added if the seller has agreed to pay it.

(c) The escrow fee will be added. Normally and traditionally, seller and buyer agree to pay one-half, but this is subject to negotiation.

(d) Liens and interests against the property which the seller must pay in order to give the buyer a good title may affect the final price.

(e) Recording fees, chargeable to the seller, must be taken into account. Sometimes, in order to give the buyer a good title, the seller must record deeds or other instruments, such as discharges of liens or mortgages.

(f) Real estate commissions and other seller's fees are also added at this point. When a new mortgage is obtained by the buyer, the lender pays the money borrowed by the buyer into escrow and attaches conditions to the payment out of these monies, such as requiring the deposit of a fire insurance policy. The escrow agent will be asked to collect the fees charged by the lender.

The lender, too, will want the buyer to have a good title and will instruct the escrow agent to look into this. The escrow agent will also arrange for and obtain the mortgage title insurance policy for which the buyer will be charged. If the seller has agreed to take a second mortgage, the escrow agent will obtain it from the buyer and record it against the property.

Don't expect, if you are the seller, that the escrow agent will pay out your money as soon as you deliver the deed; and, if you are the buyer, don't expect to get your deed as soon as you pay the money. It does not work that way. The reason is that time has passed since the preliminary title report was issued. Things should have happened as part of the escrow that will change the conditions of the title. For instance, the seller will have given the escrow agent instructions about the kind of deed to be given to the buyer, and the buyer will have given instructions on how he or she wants to hold title.

The escrow agent will want to verify that these changes have occurred. But this verification can take place only at the instant of recording. Thus, the escrow agent will send the documents to the title company for recording with instructions to record only when it is prepared to issue its title insurance policy with the condition of title, as everyone expects it to be.

All of this takes a couple of working days. So you must wait for your check. When your check is ready, go get it. Do not wait for the mail. Even a few days' loss of interest can be a lot, but what's worse, there could be a longer delay if the mail is lost.

SAMPLE #11
ESCROW INSTRUCTIONS *
(Seller)

ESCROW INSTRUCTIONS
(Seller)

T   SAFECO TITLE INSURANCE COMPANY
         OF OREGON

       Portland, Oregon

Escrow No.   1234

Escrow Officer

Date   Sept. 15, 1990

A.   I hand you herewith an executed Warranty Deed

describing land in the City of   Portland   , County of   Multnomah   , to wit:

Lot 5, Block 4, HAZELWOOD TERRACE

which you are instructed to deliver to   Albert and Ruth Jones

when you can obtain for my account the sum of $ 55,500.00

B.   From said sum you are instructed to deduct and pay the following:

1. $ none   Commission

2. $ 154.00   Title Ins. Prem.

3. $ 58.00   1/2 Escrow Fee

4. $ 15,895.00/   Pay Off ~~Mtg~~./Cont.

5. $1,499.06 street improvement lien plus interest @ 6% from 9-15-90 to closing

6. $542.54 for real property taxes and interest @ 12% from 7-1-89 to date of closing

7. $3.00 recording fee

Plus interest @ 7% from 9-1-90 to closing

C.   You are instructed to prorate as of   Sept. 15, 1990   the following: 1990/91 real property taxes, based on 1989/90 taxes of $542.54

and charge or credit my account accordingly. Assume a 30 day month in any prorate herein provided and unless the parties otherwise instruct you, you are to use the information contained in the last available tax statement, rental statement as provided by the seller, lender's statement, and fire insurance policies delivered into escrow for the prorate provided above. In the event any lender's statement reveals a deposit, account or funds for a future payment of taxes, insurance or other future payment obligations of the loan, you are to not applicable

*These are prepared by the agent for the seller to sign.

63

SAMPLE #11 — Continued

D.   I agree to furnish a Standard Coverage ___Owner's___ form policy of title insurance in the amount of $ 55,500.00 _____ showing fee title vested in

     Albert and Ruth Jones

     Subject to the printed exceptions, exclusions and stipulations which are part of said policy and to the following:
1. Taxes for the fiscal year 1990/91   a lien not yet payable
2. Easement recorded 7/5/63 in Book 542, Page 31
3. Conditions & Restrictions recorded 8/5/63 in Book 565, Page 42
4. Trust Deed in favor of Commonwealth Inc. (Purchaser's obligation)

E.   You are further instructed as follows: Existing fire insurance policy to be cancelled by seller outside of escrow.

F.   All water and utility bills and fuel oil, if any, will be adjusted between buyer and seller outside of escrow.

You will file for record the instruments and documents to comply with these instructions and then pay off incumbrances as instructed herein. You shall not be held responsible for any liens or incumbrances that may attach after such filing or recording.

These instructions shall be binding on the undersigned until the close of business on October 15 _____, 19 90 ___, and shall be performed within said period or thereafter until written demand by the undersigned is made upon you for the revocation hereof: provided, however, that your agency as escrow holder will not extend beyond six months from the date set forth above. Any such written notice shall be effective upon receipt of such notice.

Proceeds of this escrow will be disbursed by your check payable to the parties as their names are signed hereon, and your checks and documents mailed to the addresses set forth in these instructions.

You are instructed to furnish to any broker or lender identified with this transaction or anyone acting on behalf of such lender, any information concerning this escrow, copies of all instructions, amendments and statements upon request.

_____   Address_____

_____   _____

_____   _____

_____   _____

Escrow Instructions, Sellers, Page 2

64

SAMPLE #12
CLOSING STATEMENT
(Seller)

SAFECO TITLE INSURANCE COMPANY

STATEMENT OF ESCROW NO. 1234
TO Gladys Wilkins

OFFICE Portland
DATE Sept. 15, 1990

	CHARGES	CREDITS
PROPERTY: Lot 5, Block 4, Hazelwood Terrace		
CONSIDERATION OR SALES PRICE	$	$ 55,500.00
Paid outside of Escrow		
Deposits		
By First Trust Deed — Mortgage		
By Second Trust Deed — Mortgage		
PRO-RATIONS MADE AS OF Sept. 15, 1990		
Real property taxes for 7-1-90 to 9-15-90 based on 1984/90 tax amount of $542.54	113.02	
(Existing fire insurance policy to be cancelled by seller outside escrow)		
COMMISSION PAID TO None		
POLICY OF TITLE INSURANCE Owner's $55,500.00	154.00	
Recording Deed Sullivan to Wilkins	3.00	
Recording		
Recording		
Reconveyance Fee		
ESCROW FEE 1/2	58.00	
Drawing Deed		
Drawing		
Pay off City of Portland Street Improvement Bond:	1,306.80	
Interest 6-14-88 to 9-15-90	183.54	
Late penalty	8.72	
Pay off contract balance to John & Mary Sullivan as of 9-1-90	15,895.00	
Interest 9-1-90 to 9-16-90	49.44	
Pay off 1989/90 real property taxes - original amt.	542.54	
Interest 7-1-89 to 9-15-91	40.05	
Balance due		
Balance due you for which our check is enclosed	37,146.89	
TOTALS	$ 55,500.00	$ 55,500.00

E-312 (G.S.) Oregon 8-73

® SAFECO Insurance Company of America, registered trademark owner.

65

SAMPLE #13
ESCROW INSTRUCTIONS
(Buyer)

TO: SAFECO TITLE INSURANCE COMPANY OF OREGON

___Portland, Oregon___

_____

Escrow No. ___1234___

Escrow Officer _____

Date ___Sept. 15, 1990___

A. I hand you herewith an executed Deed of Trust and Note, in favor of Commonwealth Inc. for $⁵52,000.00 which funds shall be delivered to you and $6,190.00 which, together with $500.00 I have previously caused to be handed you, represent the purchase price plus closing costs which you are instructed to pay to the order of

Gladys Wilkins

when you can obtain for my account the following: a Warranty Deed

describing land in the City of ___Portland___, County of ___Multnomah___ Oregon, to wit:

Lot 5, Block 4, HAZELWOOD TERRACE

together with a Standard Coverage ___Owner's___ form policy of title insurance in the amount of $ ___55,500.00___ insuring the undersigned that fee title is vested in

Albert and Ruth Jones, Husband and Wife

Subject to the printed exceptions, exclusions and stipulations which are part of said policy and to the following:
1. Taxes for the fiscal year 1990/91 , a lien not yet payable
2. Easement recorded 7/5/63 in Book 542, Page 31
3. Conditions & Restrictions recorded 8/5/63 in Book 565, Page 42
4. Deed of Trust in favor of Commonwealth Inc.

B. I agree to pay the following:

1. $ ___25.00___ Mtgee. Title Ins.   5. $132.00 First annual premium Home Owner's Policy

2. $ ___58.00___ 1/2 Escrow Fee

3. $ ___8.00___ Recording Fee

4. $ ___1,077.00___ Loan Fee

C. You are instructed to prorate as of ___Sept. 15, 1990___ the following: 1990/91 real property taxes, based on 1989/90 taxes of $542.54.

and charge or credit my account accordingly. Assume a 30 day month in any prorate herein provided, and unless the parties otherwise instruct you, you are to use the information contained in the last available tax statement, rental statement as provided above. In the event any lender's statement reveals a deposit, account or funds for a future payment of taxes, insurance or other future payment obligations of the loan, you are to Not applicable

-6-

66

SAMPLE #13 — Continued

You are further instructed as follows: None

E.   All water and utility bills and fuel oil, if any, will be adjusted between buyer and seller outside of escrow.

You will file for record the instruments and documents to comply with these instructions and you shall not be held responsible for any liens or incumbrances that may attach after such filing or recording.

These instructions shall be binding on the undersigned until the close of business on ___October 15_____, 19 _90___, and shall be performed within said period or thereafter until written demand by the undersigned is made upon you for the revocation hereof; provided, however, that your agency as escrow holder will not extend beyond six months from the date set forth above. Any such written notice shall be effective upon receipt of such notice.

You are instructed to furnish to any broker or lender identified with this transaction or anyone acting on behalf of such lender, any information concerning this escrow, copies of all instructions, amendments and statements upon request.

_____   Address_____

_____   _____

_____   _____

_____   _____

Escrow Instructions, Buyers, Page 2

-6a-

67

SAMPLE #14
CLOSING STATEMENT
(Buyer)

SAFECO TITLE INSURANCE COMPANY

STATEMENT OF ESCROW NO.
TO   Albert Jones and Ruth Jones

OFFICE   Portland
DATE   Sept. 15, 1990

PROPERTY: Lot 5, Block 4, Hazelwood Terrace	CHARGES	CREDITS
CONSIDERATION OR SALES PRICE	$55,500.00	$
Paid outside of Escrow		
Deposits In escrow		500.00
By First Trust Deed — Mortgage Commonwealth Inc.		52,000.00
By Second Trust Deed — Mortgage		
PRO-RATIONS MADE AS OF Sept. 15, 1990		
Real property taxes 7-1-90 to 9-15-90 based on		
1984/90 tax amount of $542.54		113.02
Safeco Insurance Co. (H/O $26,500) 1st annual		
premium	132.00	
COMMISSION PAID TO		
POLICY OF TITLE INSURANCE Mortgagee's $55,000.00	25.00	
Recording Deed	3.00	
Recording Trust Deed	9.00	
Recording		
Reconveyance Fee		
ESCROW FEE 1/2	58.00	
Drawing Deed		
Drawing		
Commonwealth Inc.:Loan Fee $440.00		
Appraisal & photo fee 25.00		
Tax reserve, 12 months 580.00		
Insurance reserve, 2 months 32.00	1,077.00	
Balance due		6,190.98
Balance due you for which our check is enclosed		
TOTALS	$58,804.00	$58,804.00

E-312   (G.S.)   Oregon 8-73   —5—

© SAFECO Insurance Company of America, registered trademark owner.

7

TAKING TITLE

Unless you buy on a contract, the seller will deliver to you a deed to the property. It is the delivery of the deed, symbolic of delivery of the land itself, and your acceptance of that deed that creates your title.

a. KINDS OF DEEDS

Your deed can be any one of the following, according to Oregon statutes. All of them pass title but with different effects.

(a) A warranty deed (see Sample #15) is the most commonly used. It has these effects:

    (i)   It conveys the seller's entire interest in the property.

    (ii)   It passes after acquired title. For instance, in rare situations, the seller won't acquire the land until after he or she gives the deed. When the seller does get it, the land then belongs to the buyer under the terms of the deed.

    (iii)   The seller warrants that he or she owns the land and has the right to deed it; that the property is free and clear of encumbrances except as stated in the deed; and that he or she (not the buyer) will defend the title that is being conveyed. These warranties go back to the time of the first ownership of the property by anyone.

(b) A special warranty deed (see Sample #16) has all of the effects of a warranty deed except that the warranties go back *only* to the time the seller acquired title.

(c) A bargain and sale deed (see Sample #17) is the minimum acceptable deed. It conveys all of the interest of the seller and it passes after acquired title. But *there are no warranties.*

(d) A quitclaim deed (see Sample #18) does convey all of the seller's interest but passes on after acquired title and gives no warranties as to the extent of the seller's title. In Oregon a quitclaim deed has a limited usage. The term "quitclaim" has a catchy sound. Partly because of this and partly because it has broader usage in other states, some people will use one. The well informed buyer will refuse to accept it because it is inadequate for conveying residential property. The only place a quitclaim deed should be used is where a title has to be cleared. For instance, a person giving up an easement or lien filed on a property would sign a quitclaim deed before a notary, and this would then be filed in the official records of the county recorder's office. Future searches of the title would show the owner's title clear of this particular encumbrance. These are technical situations, usually handled by lawyers, and will not be described in further detail here. It is enough to say that a seller does not perform his or her obligation and the buyer does not get all of his or her rights when a quitclaim deed is used in an ordinary residential sale.

What kind of deed should you use? If you are selling, consider using a bargain and sale deed or special warranty deed. In most transactions, the earnest money agreement or land sale contract requires the seller to deliver a "good and sufficient" deed. The Oregon courts have ruled that a bargain and sale deed satisfies this requirement.

If you are a buyer, however, you want as much protection as possible, so be certain your agreement is written to require the seller to give you a warranty deed. Don't be misled into believing that title insurance is an adequate substitute for a warranty deed. Title insurance is good, but it does not protect against a lot of things contained in the warranty deed. For instance, title insurance does not insure the location of boundaries. But under the warranty you can go back against the seller for damages arising from variations in these kinds of things.

At the same time do not consider the warranties as an adequate substitute for title insurance. While they are written broadly enough, enforcement of warranties against private individuals may be difficult. You may not be able to locate the seller, or if you do, he or she may not have the money or resources to take legal action to straighten out your title. A title insurance company will usually treat you fairly.

As a practical matter, most escrow agents will close using warranty deeds. This is partly because of custom and partly because most sellers are unaware that a bargain and sale deed is all that they must give in most situations.

b. FEE SIMPLE TITLE

Any one of these deeds conveys from seller to buyer a fee simple title or what the trade calls "a fee." This means that you own all of the rights in the land that can be legally owned and that you have the right to pass the title to your heirs on your death. This does not mean, however, that your ownership may not be subject to a mortgage, lien, lease, or other interests.

Perhaps the meaning of a fee simple title can best be expressed by illustrating what it is not: say Susan conveys to Tom a life estate with the remainder to Charlie. Tom has the right to the use of the property and to collect the rents but doesn't have a fee simple title. When Tom dies, his life estate expires. Charlie, on the other hand, has a fee simple title, but does not have the right to its use or to the rents while Tom is alive. When Tom dies (and his life estate expires), Charlie will still have the fee simple title and the right to use and rent the property. If Charlie dies before Tom, Charlie's heirs will inherit all of Charlie's rights and step into his position as owner of the fee simple title subject to the life estate of Tom.

SAMPLE #15
WARRANTY DEED

FORM No. 963—Stevens-Ness Law Publishing Co., Portland, Ore. 97204
TN

WARRANTY DEED—STATUTORY FORM
INDIVIDUAL GRANTOR

William J. Smith and Mary A. Smith, husband and wife

_____Grantor,

conveys and warrants to Anthony L. Jones and Christina M. Jones, husband and wife

_____Grantee, the following described real property free of encumbrances
except as specifically set forth herein situated in ....Multnomah..........................County, Oregon, to-wit:

Lot 27, Block 3, UPSTAIRS ADDITION

(IF SPACE INSUFFICIENT, CONTINUE DESCRIPTION ON REVERSE SIDE)
The said property is free from encumbrances except conditions, covenants and restrictions of
record and a mortgage owing to the United States National Bank of Oregon which grantee
assumes and agrees to pay

The true consideration for this conveyance is $ 55,000.00 ...... (Here comply with the requirements of ORS 93.030)

Dated this ....20thday of ...June..................., 19..90..

William J. Smith

Mary A. Smith

STATE OF OREGON, County of ....Multnomah...........) ss.   ....June 20.................., 19..90..
    Personally appeared the above named ...William J. Smith and Mary A. Smith, husband and wife....

..................and acknowledged the foregoing instrument to be their....voluntary act and deed.

Before me: *Thomas C. Spire*

(OFFICIAL SEAL)   Notary Public for Oregon—My commission expires: November.7,.1992.

WARRANTY DEED		STATE OF OREGON,
William J. Smith and Mary A. Smith		} ss.
GRANTOR		County of ....
Anthony L. Jones and Christina M. Jones		I certify that the within instru-
2522 S. E. 122nd Avenue, Portland, Oregon 97233		ment was received for record on the
GRANTEE'S ADDRESS, ZIP		............day of ...., 19......,
After recording return to:		at ....o'clock....M., and recorded
Anthony L. Jones and Christina	SPACE RESERVED	in book/reel/volume No................on
M. Jones	FOR	page.............or as document/fee/file/
2522 S.E. 122nd Avenue	RECORDER'S USE	instrument/microfilm No................,
Portland, Oregon 97233		Record of Deeds of said county.
NAME, ADDRESS, ZIP		Witness my hand and seal of
Until a change is requested, all tax statements		County affixed.
shall be sent to the following address:		
Anthony L. Jones and Christina		
M. Jones		....
2522 S.E. 122nd Avenue		NAME TITLE
Portland, Oregon 97233		By ....Deputy
NAME, ADDRESS, ZIP		

SAMPLE #16
SPECIAL WARRANTY DEED

FORM No. **967**—Stevens-Ness Law Publishing Co., Portland, Ore. 97204

TA

CKI

SPECIAL WARRANTY DEED—STATUTORY FORM
INDIVIDUAL GRANTOR

William J. Smith and Mary A. Smith, husband and wife .... Grantor,
conveys and specially warrants to Anthony L. Jones and Christina M. Jones, husband & wife Grantee,
the following described real property free of encumbrances created or suffered by the Grantor except as specifically set forth herein, situated in Multnomah .... County, Oregon to-wit:

Lot 27, Block 3, UPSTAIRS ADDITION

(IF SPACE INSUFFICIENT, CONTINUE DESCRIPTION ON REVERSE SIDE)

The said property is free of all encumbrances created or suffered by the Grantor except conditions, covenants and restrictions of record and a mortgage owing to the United States National Bank of Oregon which Grantee assumes and agrees to pay

The true consideration for this conveyance is $ 55,000.00 .... (Here comply with the requirements of ORS 93.030)

Dated this 20th day of June , 19 90

William J. Smith
Mary A. Smith

STATE OF OREGON, County of Multnomah) ss. June 20 , 19 90
Personally appeared the above named William J. Smith and Mary A. Smith, husband and wife
and acknowledged the foregoing instrument to be their voluntary act and deed.

Before me: *Thomas C. Szjac*

(OFFICIAL SEAL) Notary Public for Oregon—My commission expires: November 7, 1992

SPECIAL WARRANTY DEED William J. Smith and Mary A. Smith <small>GRANTOR</small> Anthony L. Jones and Christina M. Jones 2522 S.E. 122nd Avenue, Portland, Oregon 97233 <small>GRANTEE'S ADDRESS, ZIP</small> **After recording return to:** Anthony L. Jones and Christina M. Jones 2522 S.E. 122nd Avenue Portland, Oregon 97233 <small>NAME, ADDRESS, ZIP</small> **Until a change is requested, all tax statements shall be sent to the following address:** Anthony L. Jones and Christina M. Jones 2522 S.E. 122nd Avenue, Portland, Oregon 97233 <small>NAME, ADDRESS, ZIP</small>	**STATE OF OREGON** } ss. County of .... I certify that the within instrument was received for record on the .... day of ...., 19......, at ....o'clock......M., and recorded in book .... on page .... or as file/reel number ...., Record of Deeds of said County. Witness my hand and seal of County affixed. .... Recording Officer By .... Deputy
	SPACE RESERVED FOR RECORDER'S USE

---

*This means that the grantor promises to defend the title against claims arising during the ownership of the grantor.

73

SAMPLE #17
BARGAIN AND SALE DEED

FORM No. 961—Stevens-Ness Law Publishing Co., Portland, Ore. 97204

TN

BARGAIN AND SALE DEED—STATUTORY FORM
INDIVIDUAL GRANTOR

William J. Smith and Mary A. Smith, husband and wife,

....Grantor,

conveys to ......Anthony L. Jones and Christina M. Jones, husband and wife,.....................

....Grantee, the following real property situated in ......Multnomah.........

County, Oregon, to-wit:

Lot 27, Block 3, UPSTAIRS ADDITION

(IF SPACE INSUFFICIENT, CONTINUE DESCRIPTION ON REVERSE SIDE)

The true consideration for this conveyance is $ 55,000.00 ... (Here comply with the requirements of ORS 93.030)

Dated this ....20th....day of .....June..................., 19..90....

William J. Smith
Mary A. Smith

STATE OF OREGON, County of....Multnomah........ } ss.   June 20..................., 19...90....

Personally appeared the above named ......William J. Smith and Mary A. Smith,..................

......................................and acknowledged the foregoing instrument to be..their..voluntary act and deed.

Before me: ......   Thomas C. Sage

(OFFICIAL SEAL)   Notary Public for Oregon—My commission expires: November 7, 1992

BARGAIN AND SALE DEED

William J. Smith and Mary A. Smith
GRANTOR

Anthony L. Jones and Christina M. Jones
2522 S.E. 122nd Ave.,Portland, OR 97233
GRANTEE'S ADDRESS, ZIP

After recording return to:

Anthony L. Jones and Christina M. Jones
2522 S.E. 122nd Avenue
Portland, Oregon 97233

NAME, ADDRESS, ZIP

Until a change is requested, all tax statements
shall be sent to the following address:
Anthony L. Jones and Christina M. Jones
2522 S.E. 122nd Avenue
Portland, Oregon 97233

NAME, ADDRESS, ZIP

SPACE RESERVED
FOR
RECORDER'S USE

STATE OF OREGON } ss.
County of ....

I certify that the within instrument was received for record on the ....day of ...., 19......, at......... o'clock ...M., and recorded in book .... on page ....or as file/reel number ...., Record of Deeds of said County.

Witness my hand and seal of County affixed.

.... Recording Officer

By .... Deputy

---

*In this statement there is no guarantee of the title. The seller is simply agreeing to sell his or her interest, whatever that may be, to the purchaser.

74

SAMPLE #18
QUITCLAIM DEED

FORM No. 969—Stevens-Ness Law Publishing Co., Portland, Ore. 97204
TN

QUITCLAIM DEED—STATUTORY FORM
INDIVIDUAL GRANTOR

William J. Smith and Mary A. Smith, husband and wife, ... Grantor,

releases and quitclaims to ...... Anthony L. Jones and Christina M. Jones, husband and wife, ...

.... Grantee, all right, title and interest in and to the following described

real property situated in ...... Multnomah .... County, Oregon, to-wit:

Lot 27, Block 3, UPSTAIRS ADDITION

(IF SPACE INSUFFICIENT, CONTINUE DESCRIPTION ON REVERSE SIDE)

The true consideration for this conveyance is $ 55,000.00 ..... (Here comply with the requirements of ORS 93.030)

....

Dated this ..20th ..day of .... June .... , 19 .90 ...

William J. Smith
Mary A. Smith

STATE OF OREGON, County of ...Multnomah ....) ss.   June 20 .... , 19 .90 ..
Personally appeared the above named ...... William J. Smith and Mary A. Smith, ...

.... and acknowledged the foregoing instrument to be ..their ..voluntary act and deed.

Before me: .... Thomas C. Sojac *Thomas C. Sojac*

(OFFICIAL SEAL)   Notary Public for Oregon—My commission expires: November 7, 1992

QUITCLAIM DEED	STATE OF OREGON	} ss.
William J. Smith and Mary A. Smith		
GRANTOR	County of	
Anthony L. Jones and Christina M. Jones	I certify that the within instru-	
2522 S.E. 122nd Ave., Portland, OR 97233	ment was received for record on the	
GRANTEE'S ADDRESS, ZIP	............day of ...., 19.........,	
After recording return to:	at.............o'clock....M., and recorded	
Anthony L. Jones and Christina M. Jones	SPACE RESERVED	in book .... on page ....or as
2522 S.E. 122nd Avenue	FOR	file/reel number ....,
Portland, Oregon 97233	RECORDER'S USE	Record of Deeds of said County.
NAME, ADDRESS, ZIP		Witness my hand and seal of County affixed.
Until a change is requested, all tax statements shall be sent to the following address:		
Anthony L. Jones and Christina M. Jones		Recording Officer
2522 S.E. 122nd Avenue		By ....Deputy
Portland, Oregon 97233		
NAME, ADDRESS, ZIP		

8

TYPES OF OWNERSHIP

At the time of purchase, consider carefully what names you want on the deed and how you want the title held. Most home ownerships will be in the names of husband and wife, and this is usually appropriate. However, the law gives many ways in which to own property, and the most common are explained in this chapter. Choose the one most suitable for your situation.

a. TENANCY BY THE ENTIRETY

This exists between husband and wife. During the life of both of them each owns an undivided one-half. Upon the death of one of them, the surviving spouse, by the terms of the deed, becomes the sole owner. No probate or other court action is necessary. In fact, a will cannot affect entirety property; the terms of the deed control the ownership.

A tenancy by the entirety is created easily enough by deeding to both husband and wife and following their names on the deed with the words "husband and wife" or "tenants by the entirety." Most married couples will want to take title in this way. Some people with large estates and tax considerations will want to consult with tax advisers.

If you have title only in the name of one spouse, you can convert this to a tenancy by the entirety by an appropriate deed.

b. JOINT TENANCY

In this situation, title is in the name of two or more people with right of survivorship, meaning that upon the death of one or more of them, the property belongs to the surviving owners. Although it has characteristics resembling a tenancy by the entirety, there are differences, and the most important one is that title can be held this way by people who are not married to each other. The advantage of this kind of deed is the avoidance of probate on the death of one of the owners. This advantage must be carefully weighed against the disadvantages of owning property with a person not your spouse, which will be discussed later in this chapter.

Joint tenancy is created by a deed with this language following the owners' names: "Joint tenants with right of survivorship and not as tenants in common, meaning that in the death of one of the owners, title will fully vest in the survivors."

c. TENANCY IN COMMON

This is created when two or more people each own a fractional share in the property, without right of survivorship. On death, the deceased's interest passes to that person's heirs just as if he or she fully owned a separate parcel of real estate. By a fractional share, it is meant that each owner owns that portion of each part of the property. Neither owns any part of the land exclusively. Tenancies by the entirety become tenancies in common when the owners divorce. People named as tenants in common are presumed to own equal shares unless the deed states to the contrary.

Tenancies in common can be partitioned by a court order with the court splitting the property into exclusive ownerships among its owners. Because most of the time land cannot be split up evenly, courts will order "partition by sale" with the proceeds divided among the owners.

d. LIFE ESTATES AND REMAINDERS

Ownership can be acquired as (or changed to) a "life interest with a remainder." This means that a specific owner is designated when the person having the life estate dies and his or her interest ends. By using this type of interest, probate is avoided. Although this is often advantageous, its use must be carefully considered.

There are obvious benefits in the various kinds of ownership which pass the title to another person on your death. These devices allow a person to avoid time-consuming and expensive probate procedures. Most often, however, between husband and wife, tenancy by the entirety is the best way to own property. This is apparent because more than 90% of the married couples in Oregon own property together in this manner.

The advantages of the joint tenancy or life estate with remainder must be carefully considered against the disadvantages. Unlike an interest in a joint bank account which you can terminate simply by withdrawal, real estate ownership cannot be taken away from someone without his or her consent. That is not all. Should the other owner be divorced, his or her spouse would have a claim in the property. If the other owner dies (except in the case of a survivorship interest), the heirs would inherit his or her interest. Each person's share is subject to the claims of his or her creditors, and each person is free to sell to a stranger. You could end up owning the property with someone you don't know or like. For reasons like these, many people believe that joint ownership with another person, except with your spouse, is not a good idea.

If your parents include you on their deed, you must consider the income tax consequences to you when the property is sold. This probably can be accommodated satisfactorily, but it is a complication that must be dealt with.

e. RECORDING

Each county has a recording system for recording of deeds, contracts, mortgages, and other instruments concerning land. If you are a contract seller, you must record the contract within 15 days after sale or face a penalty. All other recording is optional, in the sense that it is not required by law. However, good sense demands you record your interest.

The original purpose of the recording system is to give notice to the world that a person owns the property. Without such notice, another person would be able to buy it from the previous record owner as if you never owned the property.

In the usual sale, it is one of the responsibilities of the escrow closer to record the deed or contract.

To record a deed or mortgage in the official records, the document must be acknowledged, i.e., notarized. While a county recorder will record without acknowledgment by a notary, such a document is not considered as being in the official records and does not have the desired effect of giving notice to the world of the state of the title. Some counties maintain a separate set of records for documents that are not notarized. This is called miscellaneous records.

In the rare instance where a deed is not recorded, but you are in possession of the property, your possession is said to have the same effect as recording, in that notice to the world is held to have been given. A prospective buyer of the land, seeing you in possession, should inquire whether you own it, or whether you are a tenant. Possession by a tenant is considered to be the same as possession by the owner for this purpose. Put another way, your tenant is considered to be telling the world that *you* own the property and anyone planning to buy it better first ask the tenant who owns it. Therefore, all sellers and buyers should clarify the status of people living on the property.

The county recording system is not just a record of deeds, contracts, and mortgages. Rather, it is an elaborate set of records, and they are kept in various places. The county recorder keeps the deeds, plats, contracts, mortgages, trust deeds, mechanics' liens, and federal tax liens; other records are kept by the courts, notably judgment liens (judgments are liens on the real property of the debtor), probate records (by which real estate is transferred through inheritance), and all lawsuits affecting real estate; the assessor will keep the records on the property taxes. In the case of court records, a notice of *lis penders* (litigation pending) must be filed in the county recording system in order to give notice of a pending lawsuit which would affect title. This list is not complete but it is obvious that a person searching the records must look in a multitude of places to do a complete job. In fact, it is a job best left to a professional title search company.

f. INTERESTS WHICH CAN BE DEEDED

Real estate is most commonly divided into parcels — lots, acreage, and so on. This will be discussed further in the chapter on land division and land use. Real estate can also be divided into intangible interests. For instance, a land subdivider who restricts lots to residences of not less than 500 square feet has given to each lot an intangible property right in the other lots. Similarly, an easement, which is nothing more than a right to use another's land for a specific purpose, is an intangible property right. Easements can be bought and sold (unless their terms forbid it) just as other real estate can.

A word should be said about easements, particularly those where the use is shared by several neighbors. One common example is a driveway shared by the owners of two or more lots. These can be the breeding ground for neighborhood feuds if one of the owners should refuse to bear his or her share of the upkeep or obstructs it by parking cars or trailers on it. This type of problem is not easily solved and often results in much bitterness. It is better to avoid buying property that can be reached only by an easement.

g. ADVERSE POSSESSION

It is possible in Oregon to acquire real estate belonging to someone else by claiming it as your own and using it exclusively for a period of 10 years. This is known as acquiring title by adverse possession. And note, your possession must be adverse: you must claim it as your own against the right and title of the actual owner. Strangely, if your use is with his or her consent, not adverse to his or her title, you do not acquire title. Why does the law permit what appears to be legalized theft?

The answer is that the law wants to put things at rest. Most of the time, people who claim to own and use another's land do so in good faith (an honest, but mistaken, belief is still adverse to the true owner's interest). This comes about because of surveying errors, mistaken placement of fences and the like. Often these mistakes are discovered many years later. Buildings have been built, maybe whole blocks of buildings are located in the wrong place. The law gives people only 10 years to straighten out these boundary mistakes. After that time, it wants boundary questions put at rest so people will have some certainty about their boundaries and so that there will not be endless litigation over these questions. When put in that perspective, the policy is reasonable.

9
PROPERTY TAXES

Property tax, a tax so widespread it is even charged to many who have poverty-level incomes, could be the most misunderstood tax. This may be because it is computed not by the taxpayer but by the assessor, whose results are presented yearly in a bill. The taxpayer really has little idea how the bill was determined. *Consumer Reports* has called Oregon's property tax one of the most equitable in the nation. Certainly, in concept, the system is fair. Whether it is fair in a specific case is for the individual property owner to decide.

How is the property owner's tax bill determined? Each year cities, counties, school districts and the like prepare their individual budgets. Hearings are held. Notices of the hearings are published in the newspaper. One way to get taxes reduced is to attend those hearings and express your own opinions. Few people do.

Under the Oregon Constitution, the districts' budgets cannot be increased by more than 6% over any one of the previous three years' budgets. This sounds good until you compound 6% per year and find that this allows the permissible amount of the budget to double each 11 years. If the 6% increase is insufficient, then the increased budget must be submitted to the voters for their approval. Any bonded debt must also have voter approval. The budget, after it is approved, is then submitted to the county assessor, who must determine the tax rate for each $1,000 of property value. Here is an example:

Budget for School District 280Z:	$2,100,000.00
Total value of property in district:	$560,000.00
Divide $2,100,000 by $560,000 =	$3.75

Thus, the tax rate would be $3.75 per $1,000 of assessed value. But don't stop. There is more. Each parcel of property is in several taxing districts. This process is repeated for each one of them and the property owner pays the total. Your yearly tax bill shows each taxing district and how much each one charges you. The bill also shows the assessor's determination of the cash value of your land and buildings.

What if you disagree with the assessor's value? You can appeal. This is not a particularly difficult procedure and your chances are really not bad. I must confess that when I started the research for this chapter I approached the subject of property tax appeals with rather negative feelings. But this is what I discovered:

(a) There are publications and forms designed to assist the taxpayer and explain the procedures in lay terms

(b) There are people at the county and the state whose purpose is to help the taxpayer

(c) In one year, for example, in Multnomah County, of 1,140 appeals before the Board of Equalization, 633 resulted in a reduced value, 5 resulted in an increased value (yes, they can increase it, but increases are rare) and 512 values stayed the same. These proportions, of course, will differ from year to year and county to county. Much depends upon the composition of the board.

The petition form for an appeal is not difficult to understand or prepare. (Sample #19 is an example of the form used in Multnomah County.) Essentially, you should protest the valuation of either the land or buildings or both, give your reasons and present your evidence. What evidence?

You can hire a private appraiser and present his or her report. This can be expensive and cost more than any possible tax savings.

You can do yourself what a good appraiser does: obtain details of recent sales of comparable properties and compare the sales prices with the assessed value of your own property. This takes a lot of work. First, you must find recent sales of houses comparable to yours in age, size,

SAMPLE #19
TAX APPEAL PETITION

COUNTY OF MULTNOMAH
PETITION FOR THE CORRECTION OF ASSESSED VALUATION

This application must be verified by the signature of the applicant, or his attorney, and if not so verified and filed by _____ May 21, 1990
may not be considered or acted upon by the Board of Equalization.

If you wish to have an evening hearing, please specify: Yes ___ No ___

Yes ___ No ___

HEARING REQUESTED ✓_____   Person to be notified of hearing date: ___ Tess Taxpayer
Notice of Board's decision to be sent to:

_____ Tess Taxpayer _____   Tel. No. 123-4567

Address 101 Perdiem Street, Portland   Address 101 Perdiem Street, Portland

ACCOUNT # 123-45678   Year 19 1989/90

Addition Terraced Hills   Lot 15   Block 20

Tax Lot 1520   Section 101   Township Terrace Range Hills

Address of Property 101 Perdiem Street, Portland

Current Assessed Value: Land $70 000   Buildings $20,000   Total $90 000

Portland, Oregon, 19 90

To the Board of Equalization for Multnomah County, Oregon

The undersigned, claims to be aggrieved by the aforesaid valuation, hereby petitions the Board of Equalization to have same reviewed and corrected, and asks that the assessed value of said property for the current year be fixed as follows:

Land, $40 000   Buildings, $15 000   Total, $55 000

THE PROPERTY OWNER WILL PLEASE ANSWER THE FOLLOWING QUESTIONS FOR THE INFORMATION OF THE BOARD OF EQUALIZATION IN CONSIDERING THE FOREGOING PETITION:

What do you consider is the full market value (selling value of property)? $70 000
In what year was the property acquired? 1978   What was the full consideration? $60 000
In what manner was the property acquired?   Private sale or _____

Has property ever been offered for sale? No   If so, state amount any year $ _____
The assessed valuation placed on said LAND is not correct for the following reasons:

    The lot lacks a view, is low and has poor drainage in

    comparison with other similar sized lots in the area

_____

_____

The assessed valuation placed on said BUILDING is not correct for the following reasons:

    The buildings - house and garage, are old and in need of

    substantial maintenance

_____

Character of building stucco, 3 storey   Year of Construction 1940   Cost of Construction unknown
If building has been remodeled since it was built, state in what year and cost of same: 1960
_____ Is property rented or leased? no
If so, state monthly rental $ no   For what amount is building insured $ 55 000

DECLARATION

I, _____ , declare under the penalties for false swearing
as contained in ORS 305.990(5) that the contents of the foregoing Petition for Review
are true.

_____   _____   _____   _____
    Signature   address   City   State

84

construction and style and in an area comparable to your own. Then you must find out what they have sold for. You can do this by inquiring of realtors who have a wealth of information both in their personal knowledge and in their multiple listing books. The Multnomah county assessor prepares a large book printed by a computer which lists the sales prices of all sales within the county. This book is used by appraisers and is available for your use.

The purchase of your home, if recent, is also a valid comparable sale. In fact, it is the best evidence of value. Assembling this evidence is not beyond the skill of most laypeople. It takes time and effort, but without evidence the appeal has practically no chance of success.

Once you determine that the assessor has overvalued your property, you may wish to have informal discussions with the assessor's office. This is optional, and you should keep your eye on the deadline. The appeal petition must be filed not later than the third Monday in May. After that, it's too late. If you need help in preparing the petition, the county has employees who will assist you. Don't be afraid to ask. They work with these cases daily and sincerely try to help you win.

The first level of appeal is the Board of Equalization. This name sounds foreboding but it is nothing more than a board for correcting the assessed valuation. It may act on your petition without a hearing, using the evidence you have presented with the petition. If you want a hearing, however, request one. The board must decide the case by July 1.

If you lose, you can still appeal to the Oregon Department of Revenue or the small claims division of the Oregon tax court. Be careful! A decision by the small claims division cannot be appealed further, whereas an appeal to the Department of Revenue can be appealed to the regular division of the Oregon tax court and from there to the Supreme Court of Oregon.

Appeals to the Department of Revenue or small claims division are more formal than those to the Board of Equalization but can be handled by a competent layperson.

Indeed, because of the relatively small amount at issue, there is often no other way except to do it yourself. An attorney's fee could exceed the amount at stake. Either the small claims division or the Department of Revenue will give you a petition form and someone will assist you with its preparation if necessary. Your evidence and its presentation is the same as before the Board of Equalization. You can also present new and additional evidence because this is a new hearing.

If the amounts involved are large or if your appeal should go to the regular division of the tax court or higher, you will need the services of an attorney.

If you are purchasing the property in installments, the debt instrument will in one way or another require you to pay the property taxes. Oregon property taxes are assessed on a fiscal year basis from July 1 to June 30. They are billed as payable on November 15 and when so paid are paid partially in arrears (back to the previous July 1) and partially in advance (ahead to the next June 30).

Oregon law allows a 3% discount for full payment by November 15. Discounts will also be allowed for partial payments made by that date — 2% when two-thirds is paid and 1% when half is paid. It also allows payment in one-third installments with the first due on November 15, the second on February 15 and the third on May 15. Payments not made on those dates will accrue interest at the rate of 1% per month or fraction of a month until paid. Taxes are not considered delinquent unless not fully paid by May 15. Hence, payment in one-third installments or any full payment by May 15 is not a default of a contractual or mortgage obligation to make timely payment of taxes. However, every contract is different. Rely on its terms, not this general statement. If in doubt, seek your attorney's advice.

10

TAX ISSUES

Ownership of real estate is probably the only way that a person of average means can get a break on taxes. Through its tax policy the government grants a generous subsidy to those who own real estate, whether for residential or business purposes. The subsidy comes up in various ways. I will discuss these tax matters only in the most general way — each of the subjects is large enough to occupy a book this size. My purpose is not so much to explain the tax law as to make you aware that a tax issue exists so that you can consult your tax advisers ahead of time.

a. TAX SHELTER

If you own your home, you may deduct from your income the interest on your loan and your real estate taxes. If you rent this house to another person, you are also allowed a deduction for depreciation of the building. This means that the cost of the building is spread out over its life, and each year you may deduct the percentage of cost attributable to that year.

For example:

Cost:	$40,000
Life:	30 years
One year:	$\frac{\$40,000}{30} = \$1,333.33$

and so on until all of the cost has been used up. In many cases all or most of the rental income is offset by the total of these deductions and this creates what is known as "tax shelter."

What is "life" in this context? The IRS has a set of intricate criteria for determining life, including when the building was placed in service as a rental. Unless you feel comfortable trying to apply these rules (few people do), have an accountant do it.

But there is a day of reckoning. When you sell a depreciated building, you usually "recapture" the depreciation. In other words, you do not sell it for the depreciated value which is shown on your account books. Thus, in our example, if the building cost $40,000 and you have depreciated (i.e., deducted from the cost) the total of three years' depreciation or $4,000, the computation of your gain begins with your cost less depreciation, in this case $36,000. Your profit is $4,000 more than it would have been without depreciation.

At one time you would have benefited by paying taxes at the much lower capital gain tax rate. No such rate exists any more and you will be taxed at the highest marginal rate if you had enough other income. This is 33% federal and 9% Oregon.

b. INSTALLMENT SALES

The capital gain on an installment sale may be amortized or prorated over the duration of the installments.

The year of the sale means the tax year of the seller, not just any 12 months.

c. TRADES AND EXCHANGES

You may trade your investment real estate for another parcel of investment real estate and have no taxable gain. This is true even though your property has tripled in value and is equal to the one you acquire. Trades are tricky and transactions must follow each other closely. Consult your tax advisers ahead of time.

Remember, a trade means just that. There is a common belief, which is erroneous, that if you sell your real estate and reinvest the money in another parcel of land there is no taxable gain. Except for the sale of your family home and a sale by eminent domain (sale by government order — see section f. following for a more detailed discussion), this is just not so.

d. SALE OF YOUR RESIDENCE

The tax on a portion or all of the profit from the sale of your principal residence may be postponed. If you purchase a new residence costing as much or more than the sales price of your old home, you can postpone the tax on the profit. But the tax is only postponed, not forgiven. If you should sell the new residence in a later year and again replace it, you may continue to postpone the tax on any profit you realize, and so on through any number of transactions. However, should you fail to replace your sold residence, all of the profits become taxable in that year.

The gain (and therefore the tax from the sale of your principal residence) may be postponed for up to two years after the sale of the old residence. The result is that for income tax purposes the cost of the new residence is reduced by the amount of gain which you postpone.

If you or your spouse are over 55 years of age, you may totally exclude up to $125,000 of the gain resulting from the sale of your home. But you can do this only once in your life and to qualify it must have been your principal residence for three years or more during the five-year period prior to sale. It is not automatic. You must elect to do it and once having elected, you can't do it again, even though your gain was less than $125,000.

e. MOVING EXPENSES

If you have moved to a new residence because you were transferred or obtained a new job, you may be able to deduct many of your moving expenses. These include:

(a) The cost of travel to the new location

(b) The cost of moving your goods

(c) The cost of househunting trips made before you move. This includes transportation, meals, and lodging for yourself and members of your household. This is true even though you do not find a new residence, and you may deduct for more than one trip.

(d) The cost of temporary living quarters at the new location, but this includes only the cost of meals and lodging for up to 30 consecutive days after obtaining work

(e) The costs of selling and acquiring a residence. These include real estate commissions, attorney fees, title and escrow fees, loan placement charges and similar expenses. This is significant because these are normally not deductible. (However, they always may be used to reduce capital gain or increase the cost basis of a residence.)

To qualify for the deduction, your new place of work must be at least 35 miles farther from your old residence than your old job was; you must be employed full time for at least 39 weeks during the first 12 months after the move; your move must be within one year from the time you first report to the new job; and your expenses must be reasonable.

f. CONDEMNATION/EMINENT DOMAIN

When the government takes private property for a public use and pays the owner a reasonable price, this is called condemnation or eminent domain. Property condemned is said to be "involuntarily converted" to cash. A person whose real estate has been "involuntarily converted" may buy replacement property within a certain period and his or her gain will be nontaxable. The replacement property purchased must be put to use in a manner that is similar to or related to the use of the condemned property. The rules are tricky so be sure that a sale like this complies with all of the tax rules.

11

FORECLOSURE

a. MORTGAGES

Foreclosure is an unhappy situation for both sides. It would seem that a person taking back a property by a foreclosure, if successful, would stand to make a nice profit. This rarely is the case. Usually by the time things get this far, many payments have been missed, property taxes are in arrears and there is often much anxiety and emotional trauma.

Sometimes it can cause a seller financial burdens. Prior to 1980, foreclosures in Oregon happened in only a very small percentage of credit sales. With high interest rates and declining property values (or values slow to appreciate), they have become more common. Commercial lenders, who have lost money because of foreclosures, have become much more wary. If you are considering selling your property by installment payment, you should also be cautious. Do not sell your real estate on credit terms unless you have the capital and the stamina to go through a foreclosure if you need to.

From the buyer's standpoint, a foreclosure is even more unhappy. You may lose your home, your investment equity, and your pride.

One of the problems with a private credit sale is that the buyer does not come under the same scrutiny that he or she would if applying for a loan at a bank. Those evaluating the person's ability to buy sometimes do not have the credit information or experience available to professional lenders. Down payments are often smaller and payment terms less favorable to the creditor (seller).

Despite this, foreclosures occur only in a relatively small percentage of installment sales. If you sell on credit, consult with your banker and make the sale businesslike.

If foreclosure becomes necessary, probably you will need an attorney to conduct it or assist you. You should follow his or her advice and judgment. Often, in lieu of foreclosure, the buyer will be asked to deed the property back to you. Even if this involves paying the buyer a small consideration for the deed, it is usually cheaper and less aggrieving than a foreclosure procedure.

A deed in lieu of foreclosure is not just any deed. It must be done with care and with the correct language in it so that it releases the buyer and at the same time protects the interests of the seller. Consult your attorney.

A mortgage is foreclosed by bringing a law suit and getting a judicially ordered sale. The creditor (mortgagee) sues the debtor (mortgagor) for the amount of mortgage debt including all the expenses of foreclosure. The creditor requests in the suit that the debt be paid by sale of the mortgaged property at a public auction conducted by the sheriff — usually on the courthouse steps. If the sale does not bring in enough to pay the debt, what is unpaid is called a deficiency judgment. The debtor is personally liable to pay this like any other judgment. If the sale results in a surplus, it must be refunded to the debtor-mortgagor.

But, all is not over. The law in its mercy gives a debtor-mortgagor a right for six months after the sheriff's sale to buy back the property at the sale price plus interest. If, after that time, he or she does not buy it back, the sheriff's certificate given to the buyer (new owner) is exchanged for a sheriff's deed of title to the buyer.

b. SECOND MORTGAGES

Deficiency judgments are not permitted when the mortgage that is foreclosed is what is called a purchase money mortgage. Traditionally, a purchase money mortgage has been one given directly to the seller as part of the purchase price. It can be and often is a second mortgage granted by the buyer to the seller. By recent statute, a purchase money mortgage now also means one given to a financial institution for the funds to buy your principal residence or a recreational home. No deficiency judgment is allowed if the mortgage is under $50,000.

c. CONTRACTS

Real estate contracts are foreclosed by a court procedure called strict foreclosure. In this situation there is no judicial sale, no deficiency judgment, and no possibility of the buyer obtaining any surplus. Procedurally, the court orders an interim decree giving the buyer a period of time in which to pay the entire balance owing on the contract, plus costs of foreclosure, or forever be barred and foreclosed of the property.

The period of time given is up to the court's discretion, which takes into consideration the value of the buyer's equity. This can be harsh if the buyer has a significant equity, which means he or she has paid a great deal of the money owing. There is, however, a little known law that does soften this. If you have already paid a substantial amount of the money owing on the contract (a large contract equity), the court will not order a strict foreclosure. Instead, it will order foreclosure by sale and give you a chance to recover some of your investment. But this is not done automatically; the issue must be presented properly to the court, so you will need an attorney.

As previously stated, the contract seller has the best of all worlds. Recent developments in the law give the seller a wide range of remedies. Besides foreclosing, the seller can sue for specific performance or declare forfeiture.

1. Sue for specific performance

This is a hybrid because it contains some of the elements of foreclosure. The judgment of court will order the buyer to pay the balance owing on the purchase price, plus seller's attorney fees, plus costs within a fixed period of time, that period being at the court's discretion. The court will also declare this judgment to be a first lien on the real estate. If the buyer pays within that time, that ends the lawsuit. But if the buyer fails to pay, then the sheriff is ordered to sell the real estate at a sheriff's auction sale. If the sale does not realize the amount of the judgment, the deficiency is a personal debt and liability of the buyer. What's more, there is no period of redemption as there is with a mortgage.

2. Declare forfeiture

Most real estate contracts contain a provision allowing the seller to declare the contract null and void if the buyer should default. Forfeiture is now regulated by statute which creates for the seller an easy, fast, and inexpensive procedure. It can be quite valuable.

Essentially, it calls for giving the buyer a notice of default along with an opportunity to cure the default — that opportunity being 60 days when the debt is greater than 75% of the purchase price, 90 days when the debt is greater than 50% of the purchase price, and 120 days when the debt is 50% or less of the purchase price. A buyer who fails to cure, by payment of the costs of forfeiture and attorney fees within the appropriate time limit, loses his or her equity in the property and title, free of the buyer's interest, is restored to the seller.

d. DEED OF TRUST

The law allows a trust deed to be foreclosed out of court by a procedure whereby certain documents are recorded and then given to the debtor. As in a mortgage foreclosure, the property is ordered sold.

Unlike mortgages, which always require full payment of the entire balance due under the agreement to restore the buyer to good standing, trust deeds can be restored by paying only the arrears and costs within a certain period of time. In many ways trust deeds seem an ideal means for both the seller who has a simple means of foreclosing and for the buyer who can easily restore his or her good standing. However, as the trust deeds lack the protections afforded by courts in other foreclosures, they do present possibilities of abuse.

Trust deeds may also be foreclosed in the courts if the buyer is unable or unwilling to make further payments or has repeatedly been late under the mortgage, in which case the same rules apply as for mortgages.

Amendments in the law now distinguish between commercial trust deeds and other trust deeds. A commercial trust deed is one covering real estate on which the building is not designed for residential use or, if designed for residential use, is one which the debtor or spouse or child does not occupy as a principal residence at the time foreclosure is commenced. The significance is that a deficiency judgment is allowable in the case of a commercial trust deed.

12

ALL ABOUT LAND

a. SURVEYS

When you have your land surveyed, you are essentially using the system of celestial navigation to find where on the earth your property sits. On June 4, 1951, John B. Preston, first Surveyor General of Oregon, located the intersection of the Willamette Meridian and the Baseline. This point is located in Portland's West Hills near Mt. Calvary Cemetery. The Willamette Meridian, often referred to as W.M., runs north to the Canadian border and south to the California border. It coincides with Portland's 65th Avenue. The Baseline runs west to the Pacific Ocean and east to Idaho. It coincides approximately with Stark Street. All land in this part of the country is measured by how far east or west it lies of the Willamette Meridian and how far north or south it lies of the Baseline. The intersection was selected as the spot for the Willamette Stone because of the need to find a place where the lines would not run through the Willamette or Columbia Rivers, which made it difficult to follow the lines and perform accurate surveys.

You can see the intersection today in a small park known as Willamette Stone State Park, just off Skyline Boulevard in Portland.

Unless your land is in a platted area, it will contain a number of measurements, all related to the Willamette Stone. In a platted area, however, the land description as such will contain no measurements. Instead, it will read something like Lot 1, Block 7, SMOKERISE, in the City of Portland, Multnomah County, Oregon. Actually, when all things are put together, this plat description does contain measurements. When a surveyor draws a plat, the measurements of the perimeter are described, that is, their

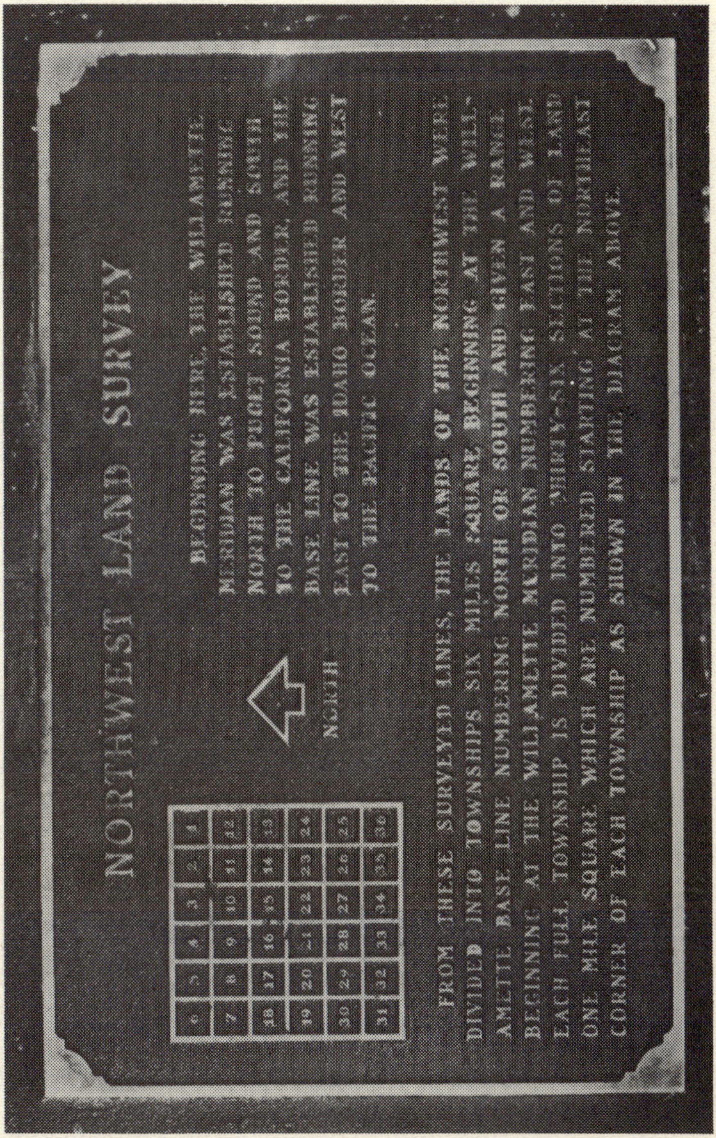
NORTHWEST LAND SURVEY
BEGINNING HERE, THE WILLAMETTE MERIDIAN WAS ESTABLISHED RUNNING NORTH TO PUGET SOUND AND SOUTH TO THE CALIFORNIA BORDER, AND THE BASE LINE WAS ESTABLISHED RUNNING EAST TO THE IDAHO BORDER AND WEST TO THE PACIFIC OCEAN.
NORTH
FROM THESE SURVEYED LINES, THE LANDS OF THE NORTHWEST WERE DIVIDED INTO TOWNSHIPS SIX MILES SQUARE, BEGINNING AT THE WILLAMETTE BASE LINE NUMBERING NORTH OR SOUTH AND GIVEN A RANGE BEGINNING AT THE WILLAMETTE MERIDIAN NUMBERING EAST AND WEST. EACH FULL TOWNSHIP IS DIVIDED INTO THIRTY-SIX SECTIONS OF LAND ONE MILE SQUARE WHICH ARE NUMBERED STARTING AT THE NORTHEAST CORNER OF EACH TOWNSHIP AS SHOWN IN THE DIAGRAM ABOVE.

position in relation to the Willamette Stone. Then such lot is measured by where it is in relation to the perimeter. The plat is then recorded in the county where the property lies. You then can describe a lot according to how it is described on the plat.

b. HOW LAND IS DIVIDED

By statute, to *partition* land means to divide an area of land into two or three separate parcels within a calendar year. A "minor partition" is a partition of land served by a road or street. A "major partition" is one which includes the creation of a new road or street, even if it is a private roadway. To *subdivide* land means to divide an area of land into four or more lots within a calendar year. All of these involve the creation of lots but the procedures for each are different.

In those cities and counties which have adopted a minor partition ordinance, approval will be required even for a minor partition. Not all localities have such ordinances. Multnomah County, for instance, only requires that minor partitions conform to the minimum lot size required by the zoning in the area. No approval procedure is needed. On the other hand, Troutdale has an elaborate minor partition procedure.

A major partition, however, must be approved by the local planning agency. This can be a complicated and sometimes frustrating experience. When buying land that has been partitioned, it is important to carefully check the partition file. Planning agencies, as a condition to allowing the partition, sometimes impose land use restrictions which cannot be found anywhere except in the partition file. In one case, a person was buying a 10 acre parcel, which had been partitioned off a larger tract. The zoning permitted one dwelling unit per acre; the comprehensive (land use) plan permitted even more; the soil drainage had been tested; and it would support a septic tank on each one acre unit. The buyer assumed one residence could be built on each acre. Yet, buried in the partition file was a restriction permitting only one residence on the 10 acres.

While restrictions created by this kind of procedure may be of doubtful validity, you must use every precaution to guard against planning agencies which are prone to lull you into a false sense of security, then later, after double checking all documents concerning the land, refuse you the right to build.

Subdivisions, in addition to the procedures required on the local level, also must be registered with the Oregon Real Estate Department. Those which have 50 or more lots must also register with the Department of Housing and Urban Development.

c. ZONING

A form of zoning existed in Europe as far back as the Middle Ages. Zoning existed in limited ways in the early Massachusetts colony. But until 1916, when New York City enacted a law specifically concerned with zoning, zoning as we know it now did not exist in the United States. Oregon's first zoning ordinance was adopted in Portland in 1918.

Today, statewide zoning is mandated by Oregon law. To supervise, and to some extent control, land use in the local jurisdictions Oregon has created the Land Conservation and Development Commission (L.C.D.C.). Under the L.C.D.C. are the various regional commissions. In the Portland area, it is the Metropolitan Service District (M.S.D.), formerly the Columbia Region Association of Governments (C.R.A.G.), whose job it is to supervise the local planning agencies. The chain of command is as follows:

L.C.D.C. — state level

M.S.D. — regional level

Cities and counties — local level

These agencies all affect the land use process. For example, in the Portland area, an urban growth boundary — a boundary beyond which municipal services would not be extended — was established through the interaction of all these agencies. This boundary acts as a collar around the Portland metropolitan area. Local governments may zone the lands within the boundary for various urban uses, but they must comply with the overall restrictions imposed either by the M.S.D. or its superior, L.C.D.C.

Another feature of Oregon zoning is that each city and county must adopt a comprehensive plan, called a land use plan, for the entire area and for each parcel within it. The significance of this is that all zoning must conform to the comprehensive plan. Do not purchase real estate in expectation of a zone change if the expected change does not fit into the comprehensive plan. The change in zoning will probably not go through. Although this book is aimed primarily at the home buyer and most persons who want zone changes are professional investors, there are times when some home buyers or owners will want to consider the matter of zoning.

If the zoning of a property or the likelihood of a zoning change is of concern to you, your first step should be to consult the staff of the local planning department. Do this in person, not by telephone. Ask the staff about the zoning of the property and your chances of obtaining a change. Their opinions, while not controlling, are an important guideline.

The law demands that notice of any zone change hearing be given to affected persons. You may approve or disapprove of a proposed land use change. You have a right to be heard and to present evidence at a hearing before the commission or governing board that determines land use policy. These hearings, termed "quasi judicial," are conducted informally but fairly. For instance, there must be no pre-hearing communications, either by you or the planning staff. If so, the decision is void.

This subject is discussed here only generally. In a particular case, you will want to consult with professional advisers.

d. DRAINAGE OF SURFACE WATER

With heavy rainfalls in western Oregon, it is natural that this state adopt rules best suited to accommodate this condition. Unlike most of its laws, which are derived from the English common law, Oregon looks to the European civil law in this situation. It says that the owner of land of higher elevation has the right to drain natural surface water onto other land of a lower elevation. In other words, you can let it run downhill. Likewise, the owner of the lower land cannot obstruct this natural flow.

But suppose you want to divert this water by channeling it into a drainage ditch or pipe. You can still drain into the lower land as long as you don't increase the amount of water, and do not change the directions in which it would have flowed naturally. But you cannot force into the lower land any but natural waters.

e. SPREADING TREES

Yes, you can cut down branches from your neighbor's tree which hang over onto your land. In fact, your neighbor could be liable to you if the branches damage your buildings; but this liability applies only to a tree he or she plants and not to one of natural growth. However, you do not own the fruit or wood of your neighbor's tree. These still belong to your neighbor. Your right to cut the branches is in the nature of getting rid of a nuisance. No court has said what you must do with what you cut down.

f. VACATION OF STREETS

You may find that the vacant lot in your neighborhood with all the brush and debris in it is really an unimproved street. You may be able to have this vacated, that is, the street dedication would be lifted. In that circumstance, title to the street would go to the abutting owners. A street vacation is obtained by a procedure which involves a petition to the city council or county council, depending on whether it is a city street or county road.

g. INSURANCE

How much insurance should you carry for fire and other casualties? This is not so much a question of law but of insurance practice. It may surprise you to discover that even though your policy is for $40,000, you may not be fully covered for a $5,000 loss. The reason for this is that most fire policies will not reimburse your total loss (up to amount of insurance) unless you insure your real estate for 80% of its replacement cost. Note that is *replacement cost;* not value. The two can be substantially different.

Suppose you are unlucky enough to have a fire that destroys the roof. Replacement cost is $2,500. Your insurance policy is for $40,000, but that is only 60% of replacement cost of the house. Your 20-year roof is 10 years old. How much does your insurance policy pay? It pays for its unused value, 10 years, $1,250. You must pay the rest. This is called co-insurance. It is a trap you must avoid.

A good insurance agent will help you. Ask for the replacement cost on the square footage of your house multiplied by the Construction Cost Index published by the United States Department of Commerce. This changes every time it comes out; so, too, must your policy every time it is renewed. Many companies automatically adjust this each renewal time.

13

CONDOMINIUMS AND MOBILE HOMES

a. CONDOMINIUMS

A condominium is a special form of property ownership. It was known as far back as Babylonia. (A stone slab contains the oldest known condominium declaration.) Its modern counterpart is governed by an Oregon statute known as the Oregon Unit Ownership Law.

Typically the condominium owner has two inseparable titles, owning not only an individual unit, but also a fractional interest (in common with all other unit owners) in the common elements. The common elements consist of the land and those parts of the building intended for common use — the roofs, foundations, columns, halls, utility services, parking lots, walkways and the like. Facilities such as swimming pools, tennis courts, and others intended for use by all owners are often part of the common elements.

Ownership of a condominium unit means that you own real estate jointly with other people. Some of the disadvantages of joint ownership are eliminated by the state law. The declaration and bylaws provide for the regulation of the rights and duties of all owners. Still, a condominium is not the same thing as individual ownership.

The Oregon Unit Ownership Law requires the formation of an association of unit owners, each with a vote, who elect the officers and board of directors. This is an unincorporated association, a specific creature of statute. The officers and board manage the affairs of the association. The association has a right to make assessments against each unit owner for the maintenance of the common elements and for other purposes. Failure to pay an assessment can result in a lien being filed against the unit of the non-paying owner and even could result in a suit to foreclose that lien.

Management of a homeowners' association is essentially the same as operating a small business. Therefore, before buying into a condominium, find out how well it has been managed by the homeowners. The best way to do this is to talk with some of the owners, and ask to see the books. This, of course, will not be possible in the case of a new condominium. You can only wait and see.

Carefully read the declaration, the bylaws and the report filed with the Oregon Real Estate Division. Determine whether you are getting leased land or a fee simple title. Carefully examine the lease provisions and terms of rent. Some ground rents start out low but periodically are escalated by the amount of increase in the Consumer Price Index. It doesn't take long for this to become pretty high.

Condominiums converted from apartment houses are subject to special rules. Oregon requires that the tenants of an apartment about to be converted be given notice and first right of purchase.

b. MOBILE HOMES

Mobile homes, while they are not real estate but personal property, are so closely associated with real estate that some mention in this book is appropriate. Modern mobile homes must meet the standards of a federal building code for mobile homes. The great advantage of a mobile home, of course, is its economy. Many people who cannot afford standard housing must turn to a mobile home. However, as good as they are, they are not standard housing, and are subject to many restrictions and cannot be placed in many residential locations. This is the real estate problem. If you buy a mobile home, where are you going to put it?

The answer is first to determine the zoning of the proposed location. The local zoning ordinance must permit placement at the location, or it can't be done. The next thing is to determine whether the location contains a deed restriction forbidding installation of a mobile home.

Obviously, these inquiries would not be applicable to a mobile home park. What we are discussing here is installation on your own lot.

Don't think that because you attach a mobile home to a foundation it is the same as building a standard house. It isn't. The Oregon Supreme Court sustained an order requiring removal of a mobile home attached to a foundation because in the law's eyes it was still a mobile home. Once built as a mobile home, it will always retain that character for zoning and land use purposes.

14

SPECIAL PROBLEMS

a. VACANT LAND

Because of its special problems great care must be taken when you buy vacant land. You must first be certain you will be able to use it as you expect.

1. Verify the zoning

The planning department having jurisdiction over the property is the place to go. Visit there in person; don't just telephone. You want to see the property on the zoning map. This is the best way to avoid a misunderstanding. But, as we will see, knowing the zoning is not enough.

2. Verify the facts concerning sewage disposal

Do not assume that the property is on a sewer just because it is in an urban area. Many urban areas lack sewers. Obtain the facts from the local governmental agency (city or county). Consult with the seller and the real estate salesperson, but do not rely entirely on their word. Many people honestly believe a property is on a sewer when in fact it is not. Most agencies which have sewers charge a connection fee. Find out how much it is.

3. Can you install a septic tank?

If you discover the property is not on a sewer, then you must determine whether it will accommodate a septic tank system. Your first inquiry should be with the local office of the Department of Environmental Quality. In most localities the local health department of the county or city is the agent of the DEQ, and its offices will be found near the planning department. Often it will have information on how the property drains, and on what is needed to install a septic tank system. If not, you will have to obtain a percolation test (called a "perc") to determine the drainage and quantity of land needed for a septic tank system.

It is in this area that misunderstandings can arise. No matter how the property is zoned, if the drainage is inadequate for a septic system, you will not be given a permit to build on it. Likewise, if the zoning would allow the construction of several residences, this will not be permitted if the percolation will accommodate only one septic tank system — you will be allowed to build only one residence. This can be very frustrating, but the state's interest in preventing the spread of disease and epidemic will prevail over most other considerations.

4. Water supply

Find out the source and availability of the water supply. Find out the connection charges and other requirements for you to hook up. Again, this should be done in person to avoid misunderstandings.

Some properties are served by a community well, privately owned and used by several neighbors. You should consider whether this suits you and the uses you intend to make of the land.

5. Investigate the partitioning or subdividing of the land

These terms are more fully explained in chapter 12. Subdivisions are regulated locally and by the state of Oregon. (If they contain 50 or more lots, the Department of Housing and Urban Development, HUD, a federal agency, also regulates them. HUD also regulates subdivisions, regardless of size, before it will approve FHA or VA loans.)

If you are buying subdivided land, you should obtain a copy of the registrations filed with the state and HUD. These contain a lot of useful information. The developer of a HUD registered subdivision must also give the buyer a written notice that the buyer has the right to rescind the agreement to buy and have the money refunded if he or she does this within three working days.

If the land you want to buy is not within a subdivision, you should investigate whether its partition (that is, its severance from a larger parcel) was done in accordance with local ordinances, otherwise you may not be able to build on it. This can get complicated because most parcels of land have been partitioned before the laws and ordinances were passed. In effect these earlier partitions are not subject to the present partition laws and ordinances on partitions. But there is no way to know this without making verification. You may need professional help.

Even after you have determined all of these things, one of the agencies which control land use could change its mind. This can be particularly true with the percolation tests. Many professional land investors will buy only subject to and contingent upon their obtaining building permits. If they cannot get a permit, there is no purchase. This is the surest way. But it may not be possible or practical in every situation.

b. BALLOON PAYMENT

It is an increasingly common practice to include in land sale contracts a provision that at the end of a short period, often three years or five years, the entire balance of the purchase price shall be due and payable. This is called a "balloon payment" or "balloon." It is often used when the down payment is not large enough to permit the buyer to obtain or qualify for a loan to buy the property. Everyone involved hopes that the increase in equity (mostly through inflationary appreciation) will be enough that, at the end of the period, it will be a sufficient substitute for the down payment needed to get a loan.

This is a risky business. As buyer you risk losing your equity through foreclosure if, when the balance is due, you can't get a loan or raise the money. As a seller you risk foreclosing and taking back property you really wanted to sell and be rid of.

Great thought and care must be exercised here. Before agreeing to this sort of deal, both seller and buyer must have some reasonable certainty that the buyer is going to be able to get the funds. You should realize, however, that when you are looking several years into the future, talking of "certainties" may be unrealistic.

c. LENDER-REQUIRED REPAIRS

A buyer must be cautious about making repairs required by the lender as a condition to its making a loan on the property. This comes up most often in FHA, VA and state of Oregon loans. Often who is to do the repairs is a matter of negotiation between the seller and buyer. If you, as buyer, agree to make and pay for the repairs, remember you are doing this on another person's property. If for some reason your loan does not go through, or if the sale fails, you will not benefit from the repairs, and you may have a hard time getting back your money or the value you have added to the property. Follow these rules:

(a) Negotiate for the seller to make the repairs.

(b) If you must agree to make the repairs, treat this as a gamble. Agree only to what you can afford to lose.

(c) A possible solution, if the lender will permit it, is for the seller to make the repairs with the buyer to reimburse the cost during the closing process.

There is a tendency when having to do these repairs to "do it yourself." With minor repairs, this should not be a problem. In the case of major structural repairs, a seller should think twice before letting the average amateur tear up a house trying to make substantial repairs.

d. DEED RESTRICTIONS

Subdivided land in urban areas often contains restrictions. In fact, it is almost impossible today to plat or subdivide without the planning agency requiring some kind of restrictions. Restrictions include such things as building size limitations, set back lines, use restrictions and the like. If reasonable, a restriction will be enforced. Rights created by restrictions belong to every lot in the subdivision; they are part of the land. In absence of a time limit or specific procedure, a restriction can be removed only with the consent of all owners of the lots, often a practical impossibility.

e. LIENS
A lien is a charge placed against either real or personal property. This book is concerned only with those on real estate. A lien must be registered in the county where the property is situated in order to attach to the land. These are the most common kinds:
  (a) Judgment liens: A judgment is a lien against all of the judgment debtor's real estate.
  (b) Tax liens: For unpaid taxes
  (c) UCC liens: These come about when personal property sold on an installment contract, such as a furnace, is installed and affixed to real estate. (UCC stands for Uniform Commercial Code, a set of laws not generally concerned with real estate.)
  (d) Mechanics liens: The law gives people who supply either labor or material used in the construction of buildings on real estate to file a lien for the amount of their charges. If you aren't careful, you may end up paying twice for some of the bills. This is because unpaid subcontractors and material suppliers still have the right to file liens even though you have paid the general contractor in full.

The rules for liens are highly technical: it is easy to make a mistake that will invalidate the lien. Whenever you are faced with a lien or the possibility of one, seek the advice of an attorney.

f. SMOKE DETECTORS/FIRE ALARMS
Beginning July 1, 1980, Oregon law requires all landlords and sellers of residential dwelling units, including apartments and single family houses, to install an approved smoke detector which conforms to the requirements of the State Building Code and is listed by a nationally recognized

testing laboratory such as the Underwriters Laboratories. The law is applicable to all persons conveying legal title or selling on contract. Penalties, going to the tenant or buyer of property, are provided in the event of failure to comply.

The tenant is required to test the device not less than every six months and notify the landlord in writing to correct any defects. Landlords who fail to make corrections may be reported to the State Fire Marshall or local fire protection authorities who may investigate and issue a citation for a violation. No penalty is provided for the tenant's failure to test the device.

The statute states that persons required to install smoke detectors shall not be liable for damages to persons or property should the devices fail mechanically.

The State Fire Marshall has yet to adopt regulations on this subject. Smoke detectors which conform to current laws and ordinances are readily available and are either battery operated or built for wiring into the electrical service. Placement of the devices is important; if you are planning to install them, consult with the local fire protection authorities to determine the number required and the appropriate locations for them.

OTHER TITLES IN THE
SELF-COUNSEL SERIES

LANDLORD/TENANT RIGHTS IN OREGON
by Michael Marcus, A.B., J.D.

This book will provide both the landlard and the tenant with a working knowledge of the laws governing their respective rights and obligations.

The information in these books will enable both parties to know where they stand and will help them decide whether to come to terms out of court or take their problems to court for a legal resolution. $9.95

RENTAL FORM KIT

Includes lease forms and step-by-step instructions. $4.95

LOAN PAYMENT HANDBOOK

This book is used when the interest is compounded monthly. $13.95

ORDER FORM

All prices subject to change without notice. Books are available in book and department stores. If you cannot buy the book through a store, please use this order form. (Please print)

Name _____

Address _____

_____

Charge to:

        ❑Visa   ❑MasterCard

Account Number _____

Validation Date _____Expiry Date _____

Signature _____

❑Check here for a free catalog outlining all of our publications.

Please send your order to:
Self-Counsel Press Inc.
1704 N. State Street
Bellingham, WA 98225

Yes, please send me:

_____ copies of **Landlord/Tenant Rights, Oregon,** $9.95

_____ copies of **Rental Form Kit,** $4.95

_____ copies of **Loan Payment Handbook,** $13.95

There is a $2.50 charge for postage and handling.